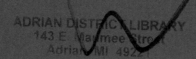

Scandinavian

HOME

**A COMPREHENSIVE GUIDE
TO MID-CENTURY MODERN
SCANDINAVIAN DESIGNERS**

Elizabeth Wilhide

QUADRILLE

Editorial Director: Anne Furniss
Art Director: Helen Lewis
Project Editor: Lisa Pendreigh
Designer: Katherine Case
Picture Researchers: Helen Stallion & Mel Watson
Production Director: Vincent Smith
Production Controller: Denise Stone

This edition published in 2016 by
Quadrille Publishing
Pentagon House
52–54 Southwark Street
London SE1 1UN
www.quadrille.co.uk
www.quadrille.com

Quadrille is an imprint of Hardie Grant
www.hardiegrant.com.au

British Library Cataloguing-in-Publication Data
A catalogue record for this book is available from the British Library.

ISBN 978 184949 749 7

Printed in China

Contents

Introduction

As a movement, Scandinavian modern shares its origins and many of its ideals with modernism, the revolution in design and architecture that expressed the machine age in bold new forms. Like modernism, twentieth-century Scandinavian design displays a similar concern for function and practicality, a move towards simplicity and a democratic spirit. Yet while many twentieth-century designs are functional, simple and unpretentious, Scandinavian modern has something more. And that additional quality has given it an enduring appeal and a broad-ranging influence.

If you had to put a name to that special quality you might call it 'approachability'. Many great modern designs are wonderful to look at. They occupy interiors like spatial markers or pieces of sculpture. Arne Jacobsen's 'Egg' chair works well as a spatial or sculptural marker, too. The difference is you would find it very hard to resist sitting in it. It asks you to sit in it.

These are designs that invite interaction, that draw people in. They often show a perfectly judged balance between the human capacity to abstract and nature's living vitality. They are quietly functional but memorably beautiful too. Technology is not on show for its own sake, but serving deeper, more expressive purposes.

In the context of modernism, 'approachability' might be considered a derogatory quality, smacking of compromise or a watering down of ideals. That could not be further from the case. Early modernists were waging war on tradition and took no prisoners. Ornament was a crime. Materials were hard and industrial, forms mechanistic, even a little brutal. What sets Scandinavian modern apart is its reconciliation of the contemporary ethos in design with the connection to nature that is innate in the human spirit. The result is a marriage of modern materials and techniques with natural materials and craft; of clean lines with organic curved forms; of basic functional performance with pleasure and emotional appeal. These are designs that show us the way forward while reminding us where we come from.

There is a moment in the fashion cycle when the previous style suddenly starts to look ugly and ridiculous. A little while later, it is kitsch. A little while after that, it is retro and charming. Scandinavian modern seems to sit outside this familiar circle. Many of the designs produced at the height of the style were classics from day one and remain so to this day.

Although the origins of Scandinavian modern go back to the 1920s and 1930s, it was after the Second World War that the style gained immense popularity internationally. This was particularly true in America, where it was known as 'Danish modern'. Danish modern struck a powerful chord of postwar optimism and dominated contemporary American interiors until well into the 1960s. After this time, the style gradually became debased by shoddy, mass-market imitations that were Danish in name only and subsequently faded from view.

Yet it has never entirely gone away. Proof of this can be seen by the fact that many Scandinavian designs have remained in continuous production, while originals command high prices in auction rooms all over the world. Those who are lucky enough to have inherited pieces or picked them up secondhand know that they stand the test of time well. Real Scandinavian modern, as opposed to cheap copies, is remarkably resilient in more ways than one. These designs were well-made to start with, but they were well-conceived too. Fifty, sixty years later and they still have an irresistible sense of freshness and vitality. It is no surprise, then, that a revival of the style is well underway, as a new generation discovers what is truly the epitome of easy modern living.

DESIGN FOR LIVING

The Scandinavian Ethos

S everal key factors unite the Scandinavian approach to design. A significant number of these have their origin in the characteristics of the Nordic environment, in the climate and the landscape. These northern countries are famously dark, cold and snow-covered for long months of the year, with brief, intense light-filled summers. And, although the combined land area of Denmark, Norway, Sweden and Finland is vast, much of it is mountainous and heavily forested. It is therefore not surprising that many Scandinavian designs have been inspired in some sense by organic forms or natural patterning. Nature, when it is this dramatic, cannot easily be ignored any more than it can be tamed.

To survive in such inhospitable conditions, over the centuries Scandinavians have developed a strong practical bent that makes the most out of limited resources and delivers workable solutions with optimum economy. When materials are in short supply, they must be used as efficiently as possible and minimisation of waste became as much a part of Scandinavian traditions of craft as a common-sense approach to problem-solving. Before the modernists' credo 'form follows function' was ever coined, the useful everyday objects produced by Scandinavian craftworkers displayed just such a conviction. Because industrialisation arrived late in the region, these traditional craft skills did not die out, as they did elsewhere in the developed world, but remained a vital part of the culture. Scandinavian modern did not shun machine manufacture, but neither did it allow the demands of machine production to supplant the instinctive handling of materials that is innate to craft. While resourcefulness and practicality give Scandinavian design its clarity, its living craft

traditions root the design process in the material world and the individual artistic imagination.

In remote rural areas in particular, households had to be largely self-sufficient and the culture that grew up over successive generations was based around the home and family life. These homes had to offer psychological warmth as well as physical shelter through the long months of darkness. They had to feed the soul as much as the body. As a result, the notion of domestic cheer is embedded in the Scandinavian approach to design. Emotional warmth is never designed out of the picture, as it can be in the more austere reaches of the industrially inspired Bauhaus aesthetic. That warmth may be expressed in colour, pattern and texture or in organic form, but there is always a human quality to Scandinavian design, even at its most futuristic.

The abiding inspiration of nature, the central importance of domestic cheer and home life, a living craft tradition, and a practical design outlook are all factors that have fed into the development of Scandinavian modern. At the same time, there is also an important moral dimension, which has to do with the political and civic climate rather than the physical one. The prevailing ethos in Scandinavia has long been socially inclusive, liberal and tolerant, which has led to the shared conviction that it is the role of design to improve life for everyone, not to pander to a privileged minority. As a consequence, simple, understated, well-made products have long been preferred over conspicuous consumption of status symbols or showy grandiose effects. Quality remains a key consideration in this preference, but it is the quality that resides in good design, emotional warmth and practical effectiveness rather than luxury or excess.

PREVIOUS PAGE, LEFT The Artek showroom in Helsinki, displaying furniture designs by Alvar Aalto. Artek was founded in 1935.

PREVIOUS PAGE, RIGHT Detail of the front door, Villa Mairea, designed by Aalto for the Gullichsens, co-founders of Artek.

OPPOSITE Interior of Villa Mairea, showing built-in display cabinets. The Gullichsens were collectors of modern art.

FOLLOWING PAGE Villa Mairea is sited on a hill in a forest clearing. The surrounding trees form a kind of palisade.

Funkis

T he 'modern' of Scandinavian modern
dates back to the late 1920s, when a
new generation of young Scandinavian
architects, particularly in Sweden and Norway,
became enthusiastic converts to modernism and
developed a style that displayed many of the
same features and shared many of the same
precepts. Known as Funkis or Functionalism, the
look was streamlined, efficient, economical and
practical. Architecture, furniture and interior
design all conformed to the same aesthetic.

The breakthrough of the movement came with
the Stockholm Exhibition in 1930, co-directed by
the Swedish architect Erik Gunnar Asplund and
organised by the Swedish Society of Craft and
Design. Asplund designed the glass and metal-
framed building that housed the exhibition, one of
the first modernist structures in Scandinavia. With
Asplund's background in neo-classicism, his
interpretation of modernism was less austere than
the work of other practitioners of the International
Style, and this was a feature of Funkis that was to
become more evident as the style took hold.

Early Funkis houses were pared-down, sleekly
fitted with built-in furniture and storage, with
smooth planes of white plasterwork, horizontal
strip windows and minimal architectural detailing
– every inch 'machines for living'. But fairly soon
the industrial aesthetic mutated into a softer, more
individually Nordic style without losing its
essential clarity or simplicity.

A leading figure in this development was the Swedish architect and designer Sven Markelius, who created the interior for the Swedish pavilion at the 1939 World's Fair, held in New York. Markelius' furniture designs, while simple and often modular, were made of wood and sometimes lacquered in bright colours. Plain upholstery was contrasted with patterned rugs. Markelius' work was more humanistic than that of Bauhaus-inspired designers, and the Swedish Pavilion gave the international community an early opportunity to appreciate the particular flavour of Scandinavia's version of modernity.

At the same fair, the Finnish pavilion, designed by the Finnish architect Alvar Aalto, was an essay in organic modernism, with its sinuous curves and expressive use of wood. Evoking the Northern Lights and the Finnish landscape, the interior featured wooden members of various profiles used vertically, setting up a rhythm that provided a unifying element for the display. Aalto won widespread acclaim for his bent plywood furniture, also exhibited at the pavilion.

Just as the world was getting a taste of the Scandinavian approach to contemporary design, the Second World War intervened. It was a time of occupation, despair and privation throughout much of the Nordic region. Materials were scarce and manufacturing often crippled by shortages. To keep hope alive, designers turned again to traditional crafts for inspiration, expressing modern progressive ideas about form and function in local materials such as timber and clay.

When the war ended and reconstruction of these northern countries began, this period of experimentation in cabinetry, weaving, pottery and glass-blowing added up to a distinctive style. Scandinavian modern's particular blend of function, utility, warmth and beauty, a product of both Funkis convictions and wartime exigencies, was poised to burst upon the postwar world.

FAR LEFT The Stockholm Exhibition in 1930 introduced Functionalism to Scandinavia. The exhibition pavilion was designed by Gunnar Asplund.

ABOVE The Swedish Pavilion at the New York World's Fair in 1939 provided a showcase for Scandinavian modern design and attracted much favourable attention.

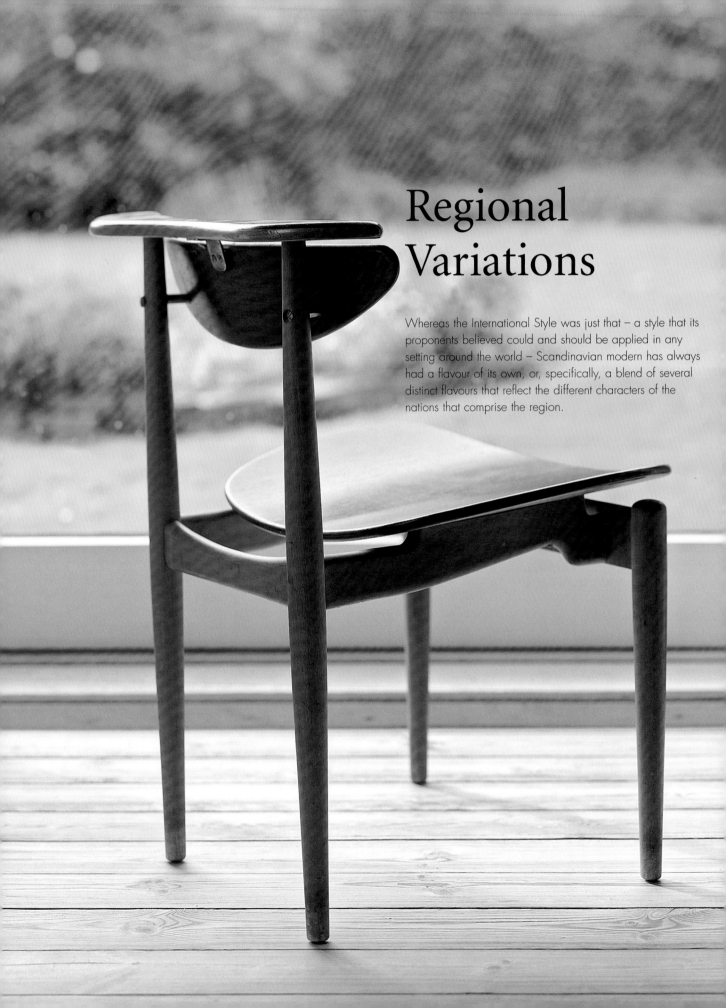

Regional Variations

Whereas the International Style was just that – a style that its proponents believed could and should be applied in any setting around the world – Scandinavian modern has always had a flavour of its own, or, specifically, a blend of several distinct flavours that reflect the different characters of the nations that comprise the region.

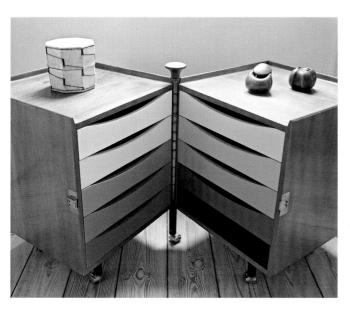

OPPOSITE Chair designed by
Finn Juhl, one of Denmark's leading
furniture designers.

LEFT Cabinet designed by Finn Juhl,
featuring multicoloured drawers.

17

Design for Living

Danish

As the most southerly country in Scandinavia and part of mainland Europe, Denmark might have been expected to provide fertile ground for modernism to take root. But unlike Sweden and Norway, Denmark never embraced the Funkis movement. Its version of modernity grew instead out of a strong craft tradition focussed on utility, coupled with a human-centred approach to design and an abiding respect for the past.

Like other parts of Scandinavia, a shortage of raw materials and economic hardship informed the craft tradition. Quality of hand-produced goods necessarily resided in good workmanship and fitness for purpose, not in ornament or the use of luxurious materials. Because the economy was largely based on agriculture, the craft tradition did not fade away as it did elsewhere in Europe and, when manufacturing became a more important sector after the war, the same high standards of production and level of skills were adopted in industrial manufacture, particularly in the area of furniture.

Funkis architects and designers had taken inspiration from the machine as the emblem of the new age. In Denmark, the 1920s and 1930s saw a different approach, where the human form was analysed in the search for an ideal design standard. Architect and furniture designer Kaare Klint was a leading figure in this endeavour and a huge influence on the development of postwar Danish design. He came up with a set of data based on average human measurements, proportions and dimensions, which he argued should serve as a benchmark for furniture design. At the same time, Klint was a great believer in studying traditional or classic furniture forms for inspiration. Both of these ideas had a lasting impact on the postwar generation of Danish designers whose progressive updating of classic forms and humanistic approach won them such widespread international success.

Between the wars manufacturers such as Fritz Hansen were conspicuous in addressing the problem of how to produce high-quality furniture that ordinary households could afford, while designers such as Poul Henningsen and Kay Bojesen promoted an organic modern aesthetic that embraced simplicity but rejected the austerity and occasional brutalism of the Bauhaus. The stage was set for the huge international success enjoyed by Danish modern design after the war, when a new generation of designers such as Børge Mogensen, Hans Wegner and Finn Juhl, taking inspiration from Klint, came up with a number of highly refined versions of traditional forms that found widespread commercial success (see pages 28–33, Scandinavian Modern Then and Now).

Danish manufacture had always maintained close links both with craft and design and the quality of the products exported from Denmark in the 1950s and 1960s, both in terms of workmanship and clarity of thought, was a powerful vindication of that integrated approach. Another defining factor was the use of teak. Denmark, a small maritime nation with a long trading history, was the chief European importer of this tropical hardwood, a surplus of which was available after the war due to extensive logging in Indochina for military purposes. While it is an irony that a heavily forested region such as Scandinavia should become known for its teak furniture, teak had certain inherent advantages as a material that made it particularly appealing to Danish designers at the time. As a hardwood, it

is incredibly strong and stable; it is also naturally weather-resistant. In terms of maintenance, it requires little finishing beyond oiling or waxing and its close grain and dark colour particularly appealed to the American market, which preferred dark-toned wood. Throughout the 1950s Danish designers perfected a number of teak jointing techniques that preserved the elegant, fluid curves of their designs.

There was another material that was associated with Danish design of the period and that was moulded plywood, a wood that could be bent or formed into curves and which was very economical. Arne Jacobsen used moulded plywood in many of his early designs, including the 'Model no. 3107' chair. Over five million copies of this design have been sold, making it one of the most commercially successful chairs in the world.

Jacobsen, like Aalto, was one of the leading figures of Scandinavian design. In the 1920s he trained both as a mason and an architect, a background that is reflected in his wide range of interests as a designer and his holistic approach.

One of the few designers in Denmark to embrace modernism, his early buildings and furniture designs fall squarely within that aesthetic. However, Arhus Town Hall (1937–42) already showed a more organic humanist version, which became typical of his later work.

Jacobsen's two seminal buildings are the SAS Air Terminal and Royal Hotel in Copenhagen (1956–60) and St Catherine's College, Oxford (1964–66). In the case of both schemes, Jacobsen concerned himself not only with the architecture, but also the interiors, furniture, lighting and textiles, resulting in a remarkable unity of effect. At St Catherine's that attention to detail extended down to locks, keys, handles, taps and sinks.

Like the best of Scandinavian modern, Jacobsen was able to combine function and practicality with organic form and an artistic sensibility. Yet his designs could be remarkably futuristic too. Stanley Kubrick's *2001: A Space Odyssey*, a film released in 1968, shows the space voyagers eating with Arne Jacobsen flatware, designed for the Royal Hotel nearly a decade previously.

LEFT Architect and designer Sven Markelius was a leading figure in Swedish modern design. This is the house he designed for himself.

RIGHT The 'Praktika' stackable earthenware dinner service, designed in 1933 by Wilhelm Kåge, was an early example of functionalism.

elite is a key element of Sweden's contribution to Scandinavian modern.

'What is useful is beautiful' was the belief of the Swedish Society of Craft and Industrial Design (Svenska Slojdforeningen), founded as long ago as 1845 'to raise the general level of taste'. That credo, which would be reformulated a few decades later by the British Arts and Crafts designer William Morris ('Have nothing in your houses which you do not know to be useful or believe to be beautiful') was a clear call for simplicity and practicality in design.

By the turn of the century, the conviction that design could be a tool of social reform was being expressed. 'Beautiful home surroundings would be sure to make people happier,' wrote Swedish feminist Ellen Key in 'Beauty for All' (1899). Key was inspired, as many were, by the illustrations Carl Larsson had published of his family life in Sundborn, a rural retreat that enshrined the whole concept of domestic cheer, simplicity and lack of pretension, its homely decoration making a powerful argument for traditional craft.

In 1919, a similar stance was taken by Gregor Paulsson, the director of the Swedish Design Council, with the publication of his influential book *More Beautiful Things for Everyday Use* (Vackrare Vardagsvara). Paulsson was urging manufacturers to turn their attention to producing simple, useful wares for ordinary people, rather than catering for the luxurious tastes of the rich and identified design as having a key role to play in this shift.

An important design reformer of the same period was Wilhelm Kåge, who designed an affordable dinner service for Swedish ceramics manufacturer Gustavsberg in 1917 and went on to spend successive decades searching for a design style that would unite simplicity and beauty with democratic ideals. Kåge's 'Pyro' range, designed for the Stockholm Exhibition in 1930 was the first oven-to-table range produced by Gustavsberg. Even more radical was his 'Praktika' stackable dinner service in earthenware (1933), which was offered for sale as individual

Swedish

Sweden occupies a central position at the heart of Scandinavia and is the largest and most geographically varied of all the nations that comprise it. Today the country is a byword for modern liberal democracy, but Sweden has a long history of tolerance and social inclusiveness, values inherent in the dominant religion Lutheranism. The conviction that good design is design that improves the lives of ordinary people and should not merely be the preserve of a rich pieces, bringing it within the reach of people on lower incomes.

The Stockholm Exhibition of 1930, organised by Gregor Paulsson and Erik Gunnar Aspland, was a turning point in Swedish design and the launchpad of the Funkis movement (see pages 14–15). Many Swedish architects and designers had studied in Paris and Berlin and were influenced by the ideals and practice of modernism. Yet while Funkis dominated in the field of architecture, decorative arts such as ceramics and glassware still drew upon Swedish craft traditions and a rival group, the Tradis (traditionalists) set up in opposition to an aesthetic based upon the machine, and what they saw as the dehumanisation inherent in mass production.

By the time of the New York World's Fair in 1939, Swedish design had reached a characteristically intelligent resolution of the Funkis/Tradis rift, as exemplified by the work of Sven Markelius – clean modern lines and progressive design balanced by softer, warmer elements such as the use of natural materials, colour and pattern. The look was termed 'Swedish Modern' by a contemporary critic, who called it 'a movement towards sanity in design'.

After the war, Swedish designers, like their counterparts in other Scandinavian countries, began to develop the softer, more organic, less austere version of modernism that characterises Scandinavian design as a whole. While the Danish had huge international success with furniture, contemporary Swedish porcelain and earthenware surpassed anything else being produced in these media at the time, while in glassware Sweden was rivalled only by the Finns.

Finnish

Each individual Scandinavian country has brought its own national character to the design movement known loosely as Scandinavian modern. In the case of Finland, the most northerly and isolated, that special ingredient is a profound affinity with nature. Much of the country is heavily forested with firs, there are thousands of lakes and in the far north nomadic Sami people continue to herd reindeer as their forebears have done for generations. In centuries past, survival for Finns meant enduring not only an extreme physical environment but also successive political upheavals and occupations by foreign powers, which has bred a strong streak of determination and staying power into the national psyche.

One of the towering figures of Finnish design and one of the leading exponents of Scandinavian modern as a whole was Alvar Aalto. While Aalto was studying architecture at a time when modernism was taking shape as a revolutionary force in design, his work never lost touch with the human qualities of warmth. His holistic approach, as expressed by a statement he made in 1928 – 'Beauty is the harmony of purpose and form' – can be seen as one of the guiding philosophies of the Scandinavian modern aesthetic. Aalto lived in Finland all his life, most of it in his family home and studio to the west of Helsinki, which he designed in 1935. During his lifetime he was responsible for the design of 200 public and private buildings in his homeland.

Aalto first found international acclaim as a product designer. In 1933 the London department store Fortnum & Mason organised an exhibition of some of his designs. Amongst these was the 'Paimio' chair (see page 45) he had designed the previous year for the Paimio Tuberculosis Sanatorium, one of his most seminal buildings. The simple forms of his furniture and his expressive use of wood, particularly moulded plywood, so captivated both public and critics that a distribution company called Finmar was set up in Britain to meet demand.

In 1935 Aalto and his wife Aino co-founded Artek, along with Nils-Gustav Hahl and Harry and Maire Gullichsen. The Helsinki-based company was intended to serve as a showcase of modern furniture and fittings and a exhibition space devoted to modernist design. By the outbreak of the Second World War, most of the products Artek marketed were designed by the Aaltos.

Villa Mairea (1938–41) is the house in Noormarkku, Turku, western Finland that Aalto designed for art patrons and co-founders of

LEFT The Finnish Pavilion at the New York World's Fair in 1939 was designed by Alvar Aalto.

BELOW The house of leading Finnish designer, Timo Sarpaneva. Sarpaneva is most famous for his work in glass.

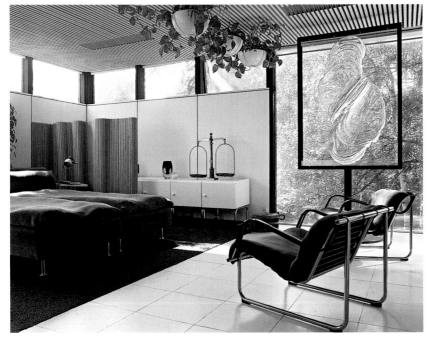

'The best standardisation committee in the world is nature herself, but in nature standardisation occurs mainly in connection with the smallest possible units, cells. The result is millions of flexible combinations in which one never encounters the stereotyped.' ALVAR AALTO

Artek, Harry and Maire Gullichsen. Located in an idyllic setting, perched on a hill in a forest clearing, the house was intended to serve as a weekend retreat for the couple and their guests. For Aalto, creating the house allowed him to experiment with a number of design solutions and it exemplifies several key aspects of his architectural work, notably the free flow of space on different levels, the use of asymmetry and organic forms and a natural palette of materials, with wood pre-eminent.

Villa Mairea is rooted in the Finnish landscape. L-shaped in plan, it is surrounded by trees that form a kind of palisade or boundary for the inner court. Balconies and parts of the external cladding are in teak, while the sauna wing is made of Finnish fir. Inside, some of the ceilings are also timber-clad, there are wooden screens and pierced balustrades, and supporting columns are wrapped in rattan. Through an extensive use of natural materials, Aalto was able to reconcile the different architectural forms he used in the building, some of which were modernist, some vernacular and others classical. An example can be seen in the treatment of the staircase. Double-height timber poles rise up through two levels like living trees, enclosing the stair while maintaining the open quality of the internal layout.

The Gullichsens were great collectors and patrons of modern art, both international and Finnish, which inspired Aalto in his approach to the design of their house. In 1939 he wrote that '…In this building I have tried to apply a special concept of form which has connections with modern painting…Modern painting may be on the way to developing into a set of forms which have the capacity to evoke personal experiences in connection with architecture.'

Complementing the collection of modern art on display in the house are furnishings and fittings designed by Aalto and his wife Aino, both standard pieces and others custom-made for the house. These included characteristic moulded and bent plywood furniture, sofas upholstered in natural or animal print fabrics and light fittings.

Finland came to modernism relatively late and welcomed new materials and technologies. Between the wars, the Aaltos produced inexpensive glassware and furnishings that could be afforded by ordinary people. A similar commitment was shown by the ceramics manufacturer Arabia, which began producing standardised goods around the same time.

After the war, Finland's craft tradition, which was less committed to the search for ideal form than artistic expression, found a new flowering in the work of designers such as Tapio Wirkkala and Timo Sarpaneva, who created expressive sculptural forms in glass for the glass manufacturer Iittala. These pure, sensual designs, which tapped into the Finnish love of nature, won huge international acclaim at the 1951 Milan Triennale.

Textiles were another field in which Finland excelled. Finnish rya rugs were the invariable accompaniment to the Scandinavian modern interior, while Maija Isola and Vuokko Nurmesniemi's designs for Marimekko were jaunty essays in colourful Op-art inspired patterning.

OPPOSITE, TOP Exterior view of Villa Mairea. Note the asymmetrical placing of the windows.

OPPOSITE, BOTTOM Supporting structural columns are expressed in the interior and wrapped in rattan.

ABOVE Interior of Aalto's summer house, the Muuratsalo Experimental House, near Jyväskylä, Finland.

Norwegian

Of all the Nordic countries, Norway is something of an anomaly when it comes to Scandinavian modern. A Norwegian flavour is not such a discernible part of the style as a whole, and Norwegian designs did not enjoy as much success or visibility, even when Scandinavian modern was at its height, as designs from Denmark or Sweden did. This is despite the fact that Norway has both a strong craft tradition and was a country where the early modernist Funkis approach was taken up with some enthusiasm.

Like the rest of Scandinavia, craft is a vital and living part of Norwegian culture. With the country's long history of domination by its neighbours (400 years under Danish rule and over a century under Swedish rule), vernacular arts and crafts, rooted in rural communities, became an important way for Norwegians to express and maintain their cultural identity. However, unlike Denmark, with its furniture-making, or Sweden, with its glass-blowing and ceramic manufacture, or Finland, with its textile-weaving, there was no one particular focus of expertise that could form the basis of a productive industry.

Norway finally achieved independence in 1905. In the early decades of the twentieth century, young Norwegian architects, many of whom had studied in Sweden, became ardent supporters of Funkis. At the time, there was a growing awareness of the potential role that architecture could play in social policy and the pressing need to address the problems of urban living, a challenge expressed in the term boligsaken, literally 'the housing cause'. The rational and democratic ideals of Funkis appeared to present an answer.

Private villas for wealthy clients also provided a showcase for the style. In Oslo, Villa Stenersen, designed in 1938 by Arne Korsmo,

and Villa Ditlev-Simonsen, designed in 1937 by Ove Bang, are both powerful functionalist statements in which the need to maximise light in the northern interior is addressed by expanses of glass brick. Bang's work in particular, however, represented a departure from strict functionalism and a move to create a fusion with national traditions. At Villa Ditlev-Simonsen, the free flowing plan is directly influenced by Le Corbusier's Villa

OPPOSITE Villa Stenersen, designed by Arne Korsmo in 1938, is an example of the Funkis style.

BELOW Detail of Villa Stenersen. Expanses of glass brick maximise natural light.

Savoye. But the use of natural stone and the way the building is integrated into its surroundings displays a softer, more Nordic approach.

Norway was particularly hard hit during the war and afterwards was left to deal with the dire economic consequences of the German occupiers' scorched-earth policy. Industry was weak and designers preoccupied with expressing a national identity. Certain designers, such as Willy Johansson, who won international acclaim for his glassware, and Tias Eckhoff, who was similarly feted for his metalware and ceramic designs, demonstrated that Norway did have a part to play in the Scandinavian modern success story, but that role remained comparatively minimal.

Scandinavian Modern Then and Now

Almost as soon as the Second World War was over, Scandinavian modern designs began to attract worldwide attention. Designers from Denmark, Norway, Sweden and Finland – four countries which at that time had a combined population no greater than New York City – were responsible for a range of contemporary furniture, textiles, ceramics, glassware and other home products that defined an entire approach to postwar living. During the 1950s and well into the 1960s, the style enjoyed phenomenal success, both critically at international design fairs, and commercially. In commercial terms, that success was greatest in the United States.

To an extent, the ground had already been prepared. In 1923, at the age of 50 the Finnish architect Eliel Saarinen emigrated to the States where he became the first director of the Cranbrook Academy of Art in 1932. Between the wars the school grew, promulgating a Scandinavian aesthetic through the work of Scandinavian artists and designers, whose progressive yet humanistic outlook had a huge influence on alumni that included Eliel's son Eero, Harry Bertoia, Ray and Charles Eames and Florence Knoll.

There are many reasons why Scandinavian modern became so popular in postwar America, but the influence of one man was largely responsible for its early visibility. He was Edgar Kaufmann, Jr., the son of the Pittsburgh tycoon for whom Frank Lloyd Wright had designed Fallingwater.

Fallingwater, by many believed to be Wright's masterpiece, was and is one of the most famous landmarks of twentieth-century American architecture, with its cantilevered concrete terraces sailing out over a Pennsylvanian waterfall. When Kaufmann chose Danish designs to furnish Fallingwater, the design community sat up and took notice. Kaufmann's influence did not rest on the fact that his father had been a client of the most famous American architect, or on the fact that as a young student of architecture it was he who had persuaded his father to employ Wright in the first place. He was also prominently involved in the running of the Museum of Modern Art in New York and a teacher of architectural history. A noted aesthete, he had an eye for both the big picture and the detail. Choosing Danish furniture for Fallingwater, the house that introduced the notion of the open plan to the United States, was no casual statement or whim. After all, this was a man who reportedly said, 'Someone's changed the rhythm of the books,' when a visitor to Fallingwater fancied a little reading matter and helped themselves from the shelves.

Kaufmann's endorsement of Danish design caused an immediate stir among Manhattan taste-formers, and leading New York stores, such as Bonniers, began offering Scandinavian products. As soon as customers had the opportunity to see what was on offer and, more important, to live with the designs in their homes, the style took hold and spread from New York throughout America.

Modernist design had previously been a minority enthusiasm in the United States. Too expensive and too uncompromising for most people, it never found an audience beyond a limited circle of design aficionados. Scandinavian modern was different. It not only enshrined the optimism of the era, the sense of progress and faith in the future, it was relatively affordable and easy to live with too. Within a short space of time, it was wholeheartedly taken up by a young postwar generation who

LEFT When Edgar Kaufmann, Jr. bought Danish modern furniture for his family home Fallingwater, the international design community took notice.

ABOVE John F. Kennedy sitting in Hans Wegner's 'Round' chair, one of twelve bought by CBS for the first televised presidential candidate debate in 1960.

especially suited to teak were to have a defining influence on the development of the style. Wegner's beautifully crafted designs reinforced the message of quality. His 'Peacock' chair (1947), a modern reworking of the traditional Windsor chair, was an early success. His 'Round' chair (1949), such a pure and satisfying distillation of the chair form that it became known simply as 'The Chair', received an almost official seal of approval when CBS bought twelve for the first televised Presidential candidate debate between John F. Kennedy and Richard Nixon in 1960. Wegner's intention was, as he put it, 'to try and make wood come alive' and in this he conspicuously succeeded.

Other runaway successes included Arne Jacobsen's 'Ant' chair (1951–2) and 'Model no. 3107' from the 'Series 7' range (1955), a stackable chair made of moulded plywood that became one of the bestselling chairs of all time. Jacobsen's 'Swan' and 'Egg' chairs (1957–8) were no less iconic.

Right from the start, the popularity of Scandinavian modern and its widespread adoption across the board meant that there was demand at all market levels. Most expensive were designs imported directly from Denmark or made by American manufacturers under licence. Slightly less expensive were the products that combined standard drawers and carcases made in the US with Danish external wooden elements. Cheaper were copies or knock-offs, some of which were reasonably well-made and designed, others much less so.

Inevitably, it was the popularity of the style that sewed the seeds of its eventual eclipse. By the mid-1960s much of what was available in the mass market bore little resemblance to authentic Scandinavian modern. Poor detailing, tacky materials and cheap veneers debased the style in the public mind until it was abandoned altogether.

If Scandinavian design found its greatest commercial success in America, it did not go ignored by the rest of the world, with many designs winning awards at international fairs throughout the

appreciated a contemporary aesthetic that provided emotional warmth along with a high degree of practicality. On the practical front, furniture was clean-lined, relatively lightweight and scaled to suit smaller houses. Pieces were easy to maintain and elegantly crafted out of natural materials. Accessories and furnishings that accompanied the look were cheerful and a pleasure to use. Here was a style that proved modernity did not have to mean throwing the baby out with the bathwater. It was evolutionary rather than revolutionary, progressive without being confrontational.

In the early 1950s, Scandinavian modern was Danish modern, as far as American consumers were concerned. Danish designers Hans Wegner and Finn Juhl were amongst the first whose work achieved widespread recognition. Juhl's refined use of wood framing and his development of jointing techniques

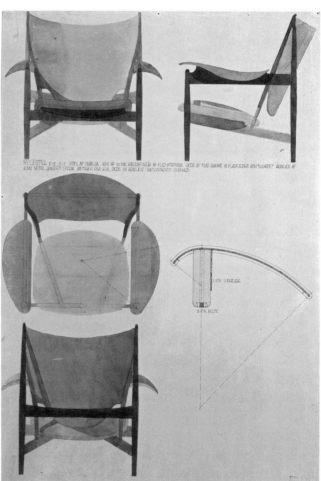

ABOVE, LEFT Advertisement for Finmar, the company originally founded to market Aalto designs in Britain.

ABOVE, RIGHT Finn Juhl's furniture designs were adapted for mass production and marketed by Baker Furniture, Inc of Michigan.

You are so warmly welcome

with ERCOL

Sit down—you won't want to get up. Relax on the studio couch—you'll feel like staying put (and in fact you can—it makes a perfect bed!) Ercol good looks give you all they promise and more. The patented shock absorbing suspension gives more resilience. The proportions give more comfort. Your room setting gives you more pleasure because Ercol give you the widest choice of easy chairs and settees any of which live happily together and happily ever after.

VANTAGE ZIPPERS
All Ercol Cushion Covers are zipped. Choose even the gayest colours from the tremendous range—dry cleaning will keep them fresh as new. A change of colour mood? Just get a spare set from your Ercol stockists and zip them on!

UNIQUELY EASY
Ercol's patented self-anchoring method of securing the reinforced rubber webbing to the frames provides deeper shock-absorbing action, unique to Ercol. It makes the perfect support for the thick, soft foam cushions.

TOUCH WOOD!
One of the nicest things about Ercol is the warm inviting feel of the subtly shaped wood frames—perfectly finished wherever you touch. You'll also bless their lightness—so easy for cleaning or changing room arrangements.

The ERCOLion invites you to send for his 52 page colour brochure and list of stockists in your area.

NAME

ADDRESS

ERCOL FURNITURE LTD., HIGH WYCOMBE, BUCKS

23

1950s and 1960s. At the same time, the Scandinavian concept of a user-friendly modernity had a great impact on a number of retailers, designers and manufacturers of the period.

In Britain, the mass-market furniture manufacturer Ercol exhibited a simplified version of the Windsor chair at the Festival of Britain in 1951, where it attracted much attention, and went on to produce a number of designs that were hugely popular in ordinary British homes throughout the 1950s and 1960s. Ercol's products did not display the same high degree of craftsmanship as original Danish designs, but they represented a similar contemporary take on traditional forms. One Ercol chair of the period, the 'Butterfly', displays a passing resemblance to Jacobsen's 'Ant' chair, although the form is less refined.

Another exhibitor at the Festival of Britain, Terence Conran, who was to revolutionise the British high street in 1964 with the opening of Habitat, also drew inspiration from Scandinavian designs, such as Marimekko textiles. The manufacturing techniques and materials in common use in the Scandinavian furniture industry was another influence on his work. His furniture-making business, which preceded Habitat, was one of the first in the country to use teak and his early espousal of flat-pack designs, which helped keep his furniture affordable, reflected a growing trend in Scandinavian manufacture. While Habitat's origins as a retail environment owe much to Conran's observations of French markets, piled high with everyday useful things, the overall ethos of offering cheerful, well-made modern design to the high

ABOVE Throughout the 1950s and 1960s British manufacturer Ercol produced simplified versions of vernacular furniture types, such as this Windsor chair.

street consumer has a strong echo of the democratic spirit of Scandinavian modern.

Germany was another country where Scandinavian modern caught on, in particular Danish furniture. Germans appreciated the light, practical and space-saving qualities of Danish designs and the use of teak appealed to them as much as it did to the Americans.

From the end of the 1960s until the 1990s Scandinavian modern was little more than a chapter of design history. But after the revivals of 'period' styles had come and gone in the 1980s and a brief vogue for minimalism had stripped the interior back to basics in the early 1990s, a new interest arose in classic modern design, not merely iconic pieces by Mies van der Rohe, Marcel Breuer and Le Corbusier, but also what is loosely

known as mid-century modern. This was aided and abetted by the popularity of the huge Swedish retail chain IKEA and its promotion of a simple, affordable, uncluttered contemporary look.

Slowly but surely, Scandinavian modern began to re-emerge from the shadows of obscurity. Many classic Scandinavian designs have never gone out of production: in fact, few countries continue to produce so many vintage designs, a powerful testimony to their timelessness. Other sources of authentic originals include secondhand outlets of all kinds, such as retro shops, online auctions and carboot sales. Prices are rising as interest builds and a new generation, equipped with a high degree of design awareness, is rediscovering for themselves just what makes Scandinavian modern so appealing.

ABOVE The huge international retail chain IKEA, founded in Sweden, promotes an affordable contemporary look that owes much to Scandinavian modern design.

SCANDINAVIAN MODERN
DESIGN DIRECTORY

PREVIOUS PAGE, LEFT Constructing L-legs, the basic element of Aalto furniture designs, from laminated strips of ply.

PREVIOUS PAGE, RIGHT Teak cupboard at Arne Jacobsen's house in Klampenborg, Denmark.

Aino Aalto

FINNISH ARCHITECT AND DESIGNER (1894–1949)

Born in Helsinki, Aino Aalto (née Marsio) studied architecture at the Polytechnic (now the Helsinki Institute of Technology), graduating in 1920. After qualifying, she worked in Helsinki for a while, then moved to Jyväskylä, a town in central Finland, where in 1924 she was employed by Alvar Aalto as an assistant in his architectural practice. They married the same year.

Described as a 'practical, modern woman' Aino was four years older than her husband and had travelled extensively. Their marriage, which was cut short by her early death, was a close collaboration, Aino sharing many of Aalto's interests and participating both in his projects and in his researches into bentwood techniques.

When the couple moved to Turku in 1927, a busy port with good connections to mainland Europe, after Aalto won an architectural competition, they were both exposed to the new movement Funkis or Functionalism. In Aino's case that influence can clearly be seen in the design of her 'Wave View' (Bölgeblick) glassware, which is still in production today.

By 1933, Aalto was enjoying greater success, both as an architect and furniture designer, and the couple moved to Helsinki with their two children. Here they co-designed and built a house in the Munkkiniemi district (1935–6), which also served as their office and workshop.

In 1935 Aino, along with her husband, Marie Gullichsen and Nils-Gustav Hahl, founded Artek, the company set up to produce the radical new furniture in bent and moulded plywood that the Aaltos had been experimenting with. Aino continued to collaborate with her husband on many of his projects and designed furniture herself for the company.

AALTO GLASSWARE (1932)
MANUFACTURER: Iittala (since 1988)
SPECIFICATION: Pressed glass.

Aino's glassware, originally called 'Wave View' (Bölgeblick) was the winning entry in a competition sponsored by the Karhula glassworks after Finland repealed its prohibition laws in 1932. The original range included tumblers, bowls, dishes and a pitcher and was put into production in 1934. Since 1988 the range, renamed Aalto, has been produced by Iittala.

A classic of modernist design, the glassware range demonstrated that utilitarian articles, mass-produced cheaply, could be beautiful as well as practical. The designs have a weight to them and their ribbed contours sit easily in the hand. Unlike blown glass, which results in seamless pure shapes, pressed glass manufacture is necessarily less perfect. The ribbing disguises that as well as giving a certain organic quality to what are essentially very simple forms.

RIGHT Interior of Alvar and Aino Aalto's house in Riihitie, Helsinki. A photograph of Aino is on the piano.

LEFT Aalto's summerhouse, the
Muuratsalo Experimental House, near
Jyväskylä, Finland, with its expressive
use of timber.

Alvar Aalto

FINNISH ARCHITECT AND DESIGNER
(1898–1976)

'We should work for simple, good, undecorated
things, but things which are in harmony with
the human being and organically suited to the
little man in the street.' ALVAR AALTO, FROM A
SPEECH GIVEN IN LONDON, 1957

Hugo Alvar Henrik Aalto was born in Kuortane,
a small village in western Finland. His father
was a Finnish-speaking surveyor; his mother a
Swedish-speaking postal clerk. When Aalto
was five, the family moved to Jyväskylä, a grid-
plan town in central Finland surrounded by hills
and lakes.

At grammar school Aalto excelled at
drawing and after he graduated at the age of
18 decided he wanted to become an
architect. That necessitated a move to Helsinki
to pursue his studies at the Polytechnic (now the
Helsinki Institute of Technology), which at that
time was the only place where architecture was
taught in Finland.

Aalto's student days were marked by
political upheaval. Finland eventually won its
independence from Sweden in 1917 after a
civil war in which many students fought. After
Aalto qualified as an architect in 1921 he found
little work in Helsinki, where established
practitioners gained most of the new
commissions and two years later he moved back
to his boyhood town, where he set up an office.

In 1924 Aino Marsio came to work for
Aalto as his assistant and later the same year
they married, the beginning of a fruitful
collaboration that was cut short by her early
death. Their honeymoon was spent in
Switzerland and Italy; Mediterranean culture
was to be a lasting influence on Aalto's work.

The subsequent three years were a busy time.
Aalto had designed his first pieces of furniture
before he had qualified as an architect. An early
commission, to refurbish six churches, involved
the design of various artefacts, including furniture.

Many of these early pieces were historicist in
style. At the same time, the Aaltos were engaged
in experiments in bending wood, research that
would inform the design of the radical new
furniture later produced by their company Artek.

Like any young architect eager for a
significant commission, Aalto entered many
competitions. In 1927 he won one to design a
building for the Southwestern Finland
Agricultural Cooperative in Turku, which led to
him moving his practice to that city. Turku, a
bustling harbour that had good communications
with mainland Europe, exposed the Aaltos to
the emergent Funkis movement, Scandinavia's
version of modernism. A key influence was the
designer Erik Bryggman, with whom Aalto co-
designed the Turku 700th Anniversary Exhibition
in a bold modernist style. He also had contact
with Gunnar Asplund and Sven Markelius,
standard-bearers for the Funkis style in Sweden
and was a close friend of László Moholy-Nagy,
who taught at the Bauhaus. In 1929 Aalto
attended the second congress of the CIAM
(Congrès Internationaux d'Architecture Moderne)
in Frankfurt.

Three major projects from this period display
a shift of design sensibility from Nordic
classicism to modernity. The Turun Sanomat
Building, the commission that had prompted the
Aaltos' move to Turku, is thoroughly functional in
style. Viipuri Library, completed in 1935,
demonstrates the humanistic approach that would
characterise his take on modernism: clarity and
simplicity expressed in natural materials, flowing
lines and colour.

Aaltos' seminal building, however, is Paimio
Sanatorium (1929–33), a commission that was
also the result of him winning a competition. The
sanatorium for tuberculosis patients is clearly
modernist and functional, with its use of
concrete, horizontal strip windows and metal
detailing. At the same time, its asymmetrical
elements, flowing forms and careful setting in the
landscape reveal an organic quality that softens
that which might otherwise be severe. Treatment

Alvar Aalto

for patients focused on exposure to sunlight and fresh air and the south-facing sun balconies are a striking feature of the wing of the building devoted to patients' accommodation.

Aalto designed most of the sanatorium's furniture, fittings and details, including a wardrobe that was raised to facilitate cleaning and had rounded corners to enable patients to move about more easily in their small rooms. Amongst other designs were a special lounge chair for the sun balconies (complete with a sheepskin sleeping bag so patients could take the air in winter) and a wooden armchair for the foyer. What subsequently became known as the 'Paimio' chair, an essay in curves made of moulded birch and bent ply, was originally designed for the lecture hall.

Like other modernist-inspired designers, Aalto had produced furniture designs in metal (he also bought 'Breuer' chairs for his own home), but he increasingly gravitated towards wood, which was in abundant local supply. From 1929 he and Aino had been joined in their researches into moulding and bending wood by Otto Korhonen, a technical director of a Turku furniture factory. During subsequent decades Aalto was granted patents on several of his inventions in a number of countries.

When some of the Paimio chairs were exhibited in 1933 at Fortnum & Mason's in London, Aalto gained his first international recognition. The modern, functional designs, which were at the same time infused with warmth and approachability, were a critical success. Sales were good, too, a factor that prompted the Aaltos to found their own manufacturing company, Artek, in 1935. In Britain, Aalto designs were sold by the company's subsidiary, Finmar.

By this time the Aaltos had moved to Helsinki, where they designed and built a house and workshop in Munkkiniemi. The project was a prototype for ideas Aalto would later develop in Villa Mairea (see pages 9–10, 12–13, 23–25), the house he designed for one

of Artek's co-founders, Maire Gullichsen.

What eventually brought Aalto worldwide acclaim as an architect, however, was the Finnish Pavilion that he designed for the World's Fair in New York in 1939 and where some of his furniture designs were also exhibited. Frank Lloyd Wright described the Pavilion as a 'work of genius'.

The Aaltos spent the war years in the United States, where Aalto was a visiting professor at Massachusetts Institute of Technology (MIT) in Cambridge, Massachusetts, for which institution he later designed a student dormitory. He became much concerned with social planning and investigated prefabrication as a possible solution to the reconstruction that would be needed after the war. In the late 1940s, after winning a number of Finnish architectural competitions, the Aaltos returned to Helsinki.

In 1949 Aino died. Three years later Aalto married again, to architect Elissa Mäkiniemi. It was to be another creative partnership. In 1957 they designed the 'Experimental House' in Muuratsalo, a cottage where they spent their summers. Here Aalto painted and designed a speedboat for himself.

After the war Aalto continued to develop his version of organic modernism and adopted a new material vocabulary based around the use of brick, going so far as to design a new type of

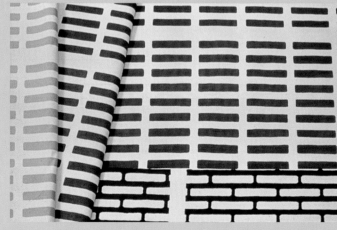

ABOVE Aalto-designed textiles for Artek.

BELOW The versatile Aalto stool used as a bedside table. Aalto's tea trolley is placed by the window.

brick that could be used to create flowing expressive forms. The majority of his postwar buildings are situated in Finland. Notable examples from this phase of his career include Säynätsalo Town Hall (1949–52) and Finlandia Hall (1962–1971) in Helsinki, where the rippled façade of the hall echoes the surrounding trees.

One of the best known Finns, whose portrait features on the country's banknotes, Aalto was a prolific and inventive designer in a whole range of fields, from buildings to master planning, from furniture and lighting to glassware. He was also an influential speaker and writer, whose holistic, human approach and embrace of nature lies at the heart of Scandinavian modern.

ARTEK

Artek was founded in Helsinki in 1935 to sell and promote the furniture, lamps and textiles designed by Alvar Aalto. From the outset, the company had its sights fixed on the international market, where Aalto's furniture had already met with critical acclaim and a certain degree of popular success. This was especially true in Britain, where an exhibition of Finnish design, including some of Aalto's work, had been held at the London store Fortnum & Mason's in 1933.

Along with Aalto, the co-founders of Artek were his wife Aino, Nils-Gustav Hahl and Marie Gullichsen. The company was not solely intended as a commercial enterprise, it was also set up to

Alvar Aalto

promote Modernism in a wider sense, to showcase the new radical style and to serve as a forum for discussion and other events.

Artek's stated design philosophy is to bring 'a human perspective to modernism'. The experiments in bending and laminating wood carried out by Aalto, his wife Aino, and his colleague Otto Korhonen in the early 1930s, allowed Aalto to combine the purity and functionalism of modernism with the warmth of wood. At the same time, he was interested in producing furniture with the fewest number of elements, not simply for clarity and simplicity but also for ease of manufacture and reduced cost. One of his greatest innovations in this regard was the L-leg, a strong bentwood support that could be screwed directly to the underside of tables or chairs, thus obviating the need for a structural framework or complicated jointing. The 'L-leg' range of designs was succeeded by the 'Y-leg' range in the 1940s and the 'X-leg' in the 1950s. These standardised elements, which could be applied across a range of designs, also had strong form-giving properties.

'Form follows function' was the firm belief of early modernists. What made Aalto unique was that he understood there was more to the equation than that. 'Form is a mystery that defies description but brings people pleasure,' was how he put it and his fluid organic designs offer more than the mere servicing of practical need.

Almost all the designs marketed by Artek are by Alvar or Aino Aalto. In recent years, however, the company has also taken on new designers working in a similar idiom. Quality is a prime consideration. Many original pieces sold by the company in the 1930s are still in use; replacement parts are kept available. The furniture is still made by Korhonen's company.

THE L-LEG PRODUCTION PROCESS
Despite a certain degree of computerised updating, the construction of the L-leg is still based on techniques devised by Aalto in the early 1930s. The raw material is Finnish birch wood, carefully selected for quality. Timber is left to dry naturally for six months in open storage, then cross-cut and sawn. Only wood that is free from any structural weaknesses is then chosen.

The solid timber is then sawn in the direction of the fibres so that it forms a fan-shape. Thin pieces of birch veneer are glued into the grooves, enabling the wood to be bent through 90 degrees with the aid of heat and steam.

The bentwood leg piece is subsequently dried in a chamber controlled by computer to ensure a precise final level of moisture. Then it is cleaned, sawn to the correct dimensions before being sanded and finished by hand. The last stage is lacquering and polishing.

WALL LAMP A910
MANUFACTURER: Artek
SPECIFICATION: Metal painted white.

Aalto produced a number of designs for light fittings, all of which were conceived within the context of specific buildings. This wall lamp, which diffuses the light through stepped metal bands, bears a striking resemblance to the ribbed form of Aino's 'Wave View' glassware.

Alvar Aalto

AALTO (SAVOY) VASE (1937)
MANUFACTURER: Originally Karhula, now produced by Iittala
SPECIFICATION: Glass; available in different widths and colours, the most popular being an intense blueberry blue and clear.

Aalto designed this iconic vase to be exhibited at the 1937 World's Fair in Paris. There are a number of theories about the origin of its rippling organic form. Its original title 'The Eskimo Woman's Leather Breeches' gives little away; most assume that the profile was inspired by Finnish lakes. However, another antecedent could be a design created by his wife Aino, four years earlier. Her vase had a wave-like base so that flowers of different lengths could be displayed together. The form of the vase invites you to choose how to use it – with flowers or without, singly or clustered as a group.

LEFT Savoy vase and original wooden mould.

Alvar Aalto

STOOL, MODEL NO. 60 (1932–3)
MANUFACTURER: Artek
SPECIFICATION: Lacquered birch; also available stained white or black. Seat options include: birch veneer, linoleum, laminate, upholstered (Artek fabric, customer's fabric or leather).

One of the best-known of all Aalto's works, this three-legged stool makes use of the bent L-leg that was the product of his researches with Korhonen. The L-leg – or as Aalto called it, 'the little sister of the architectonic column' – can be attached directly to the underside of the seat, thus doing away with a supporting framework. Economical to manufacture, it is a feature of many similar designs for chairs and seat furniture designed by Aalto.

The stool was originally designed for the Viipuri Library. Its versatility continues to be widely appreciated today – it can used as an occasional seat or side table, and stacks readily.

TEA TROLLEY, MODEL NO. 98 (1935–6)
MANUFACTURER: Artek
SPECIFICATION: Lacquered birch; currently produced (as 'Tea trolley 901') with white wheels and top and shelf covered in black linoleum or white laminate.

Aalto's genius for reducing furniture to its purest form is displayed in the design of this tea trolley, which dates from the early years of Artek. Its satisfying sculptural simplicity invites interaction. Aalto's preference for wood over tubular metal is defiantly expressed here – the flat discs of the wheels have warmth and tactility.

ARMCHAIR, MODEL NO. 406 (1938–9)
MANUFACTURER: Artek
SPECIFICATION: Lacquered birch; upholstery available in linen webbing, quilted canvas, leather and quilted leather.

This armchair is a variation on a chaise-longue that Aalto designed for the 1937 World's Fair in Paris. The frame is characteristically made of bent birch, while the seat and the back are formed by webbing. Many of Aalto's designs have been widely copied and this chair is no exception.

PAIMIO CHAIR, MODEL NO. 41 (1931–2)
MANUFACTURER: Artek
SPECIFICATION: Solid birch bentwood framework, seat and back in laminated birch ply.

This striking scrolled design, produced initially for the Paimio Sanatorium, where it was used in the lecture hall, was one of the items of furniture that was exhibited in London, Paris and New York in the early 1930s, winning Aalto international recognition. A product of Aalto and Korhonen's experiments with bentwood techniques, the chair is elegant, comfortable and easy to mass-produce. The single undulating piece of laminated ply that forms the back and seat is hung from a solid birch bentwood frame. The form is particularly dramatic in silhouette, where it seems to dematerialise into a series of fluid lines.

Although Aalto produced some early furniture designs in metal, he appreciated wood for its warmth and human quality, a preference Mies van der Rohe was said to have dismissively explained as arising from the fact that Aalto 'lived in a forest'. Yet it was just this marriage of modernity's clarity and simplicity with organic form and natural materials that made Aalto's work so popular and influential.

Eero Aarnio

BELOW Eero Aarnio's summerhouse, showing a suspended 'Bubble' chair, his first best-selling design.

FINNISH INTERIOR AND INDUSTRIAL DESIGNER B. 1932

Born in Helsinki, Eero Aarnio studied at the Institute of Industrial Arts in the same city between 1954 and 1957. In 1962 he set up his own design practice, specialising mainly in interior, industrial and furniture design; over the years he has also worked as a photographer and graphic designer.

Although Aarnio was trained within the Scandinavian tradition, and produced early furniture designs in natural materials, some of which were hand-crafted, during the early 1960s he turned his attention to the exciting possibilities offered by plastics technology. At that time, the use of plastic in furniture design was revolutionary. Aarnio's 'Ball' chair (1963) and 'Bubble' chair (1968) came to epitomise the swinging Sixties and the futuristic space-age aesthetic, so much so that they appeared in many photo shoots and science fiction films. They are still in production today.

Other key Aarnio designs are the 'Pony' seat (1973) and the 'Pastilli' chair (1967), both of which are colourful, playful explorations of the concept of what a seat can be. More recent work has included acrylic tables and metal door furniture.

BUBBLE CHAIR (1968)

MANUFACTURER: Originally Asko, now Adelta
SPECIFICATION: Moulded acrylic; steel ring; metal suspension. Upholstered seat cushions.

After the success of the Ball chair, Aarnio wanted to make a transparent version. This led him to investigate the possibilities offered by acrylic, a material that can be heated and blown into shape. After contacting the manufacturer of domed acrylic skylights, he established that the design was technically feasible and the same company went on to produce the Bubble. Aarnio could not find a visually pleasing way of making a clear pedestal, which is why the chair is designed to be suspended from the ceiling.

Eero Aarnio

BALL CHAIR (1963)

MANUFACTURER: Originally Asko, now produced by Adelta
SPECIFICATION: Fibreglass ball mounted on a swivelling metal base. Upholstered with foam/fibre infill.
ORIGINAL COLOURS: White, red, black and orange.

The 'Ball' chair – or 'Globe' as it is sometimes known – came about when Aarnio was living in his first married home and lacked a 'big chair'. During the course of its design, the form became simpler and simpler. The height was determined by pinning a full scale drawing on the wall and getting his wife to track where his head moved as he pretended to sit in it. The prototype, made by Aarnio out of plywood, moulded with wet paper and laminated with fibreglass, was spotted by managers from the furniture company Asko when they came to visit. Three years later the chair was the sensation of the 1966 Cologne international furniture fair.

Aarnio's own 'Ball' chair has a telephone inside it; others have installed speakers. The softened acoustic and the sense of enclosure generate a unique seating experience.

Kay Bojesen

DANISH DESIGNER
(1886–1958)

'Even though an old proverb says, "too much special knowledge makes you stupid" I, as a craftsman, must say that having gone through an apprenticeship in the field of applied art, gives me certain advantages in the difficult art of design, as compared to those who partly or completely work from theoretical knowledge.'
KAY BOJESEN

Best-known internationally for a range of wooden toys he designed in the 1950s, Kay Bojesen was a leading figure in Danish design. Like many practitioners of Scandinavian modern, he had a sound background in craft and an instinctive appreciation of the potential offered by different materials. He originally trained as a silversmith at Georg Jensen's workshop and later spent time in Germany and Paris working in the same discipline. In 1913 he set up his own workshop in Copenhagen, producing decorative pieces in metal. By 1931, however, when he helped to set up Den Permanente, a showcase for Danish contemporary design, he was a convert to the modernist cause.

Throughout the 1930s, 1940s and 1950s, Bojesen's workshop produced flatware and other metalware pieces, both by himself and by other Danish designers such as Finn Juhl. One of Bojesen's most acclaimed designs was his 'Grand Prix' cutlery. Designed in 1938, the flatware bears all the hallmarks of Scandinavian modern with its simplicity and organic curves; the name comes from the fact that the design won a Grand Prix at Milan in 1951. The following year Bojesen was appointed silversmith to the King of Denmark.

Despite his long interest in metalware and background in silversmithing, Bojesen is best remembered today for a series of charming wooden toys that he designed in the 1950s, and some of which are still in production, manufactured by the Danish company Rosendahl. Many are of these are toy animals – hippo, bear, elephant, zebra – of which the best-known is a monkey. But he also designed a well-loved rocking horse, as well as toy guardsmen, toy trains and cars.

LEFT Toy guardsmen from Bojesen's well-loved range of wooden toys.

MONKEY (1951)
MANUFACTURER: Rosendahl
SPECIFICATION: Moveable head and limbs; made of teak and African limbawood; available in two sizes.

Generations of children and the young at heart have fallen for the cheeky Bojesen monkey. A classic example of the way Scandinavian modern distils form to its essence, without losing the human qualities of warmth and humour, the Monkey is beautifully crafted and imbued with personality. The head and limbs can be moved so the monkey can be arranged into different positions. It is a permanent fixture on Danish television as a mascot for wildlife programmes and is given as a prize in quiz shows.

Bojesen's 'Elephant', 'Bear' and 'Rocking Horse' are also still in production and manufactured by Rosendahl.

Kay Bojesen

Nanna Ditzel

DANISH FURNITURE, TEXTILE AND JEWELLERY DESIGNER (1923–2005)

One of the few women to achieve fame as a designer in her native country, Nanna Ditzel (née Hauberg) was born in Copenhagen and went on to enjoy a fruitful career that spanned five decades. After studying cabinet-making at the Richards School, she trained as a furniture designer first under Kaare Klint at the Royal Academy of Fine Arts and subsequently at the School for Applied Arts, where she was taught by Peter Hvidt, amongst others. Here she met her husband, Jørgen Ditzel, who had trained as an upholsterer. The couple established a design studio in 1946 and continued to work together on a number of designs until Jørgen's premature death in 1961.

During the 1950s both Ditzels created jewellery for Georg Jensen; designs that featured rippling organic forms won them medals at the Milan Triennale in 1954. They were also producing furniture. Among the more popular and best-known works from this period are the 'Hanging' or 'Hammock' chair (1957) and the 'Ring' chair (1957), as well as a series of stackable children's furniture.

After Jørgen's death, Ditzel began to experiment with other materials, including foam and fibreglass. She also designed textiles, notably 'Hallingdal' (1964), a subtle tweedy fabric in a wide range of solid colours, which remains in production today and is the favoured choice for upholstering many classic modern designs. 'Hallingdal' is produced by the Danish company Kvadrat.

In 1968 Ditzel married Kurt Heide and the couple moved to England, where they established international furniture company Interspace and where Ditzel continued to market her designs. In 1986 after Heide's death, Ditzel returned to Copenhagen. Although she was by this time in her early eighties, she began to work with a leading Danish furniture manufacturer, Frederica, designing dramatic plywood pieces including 'Bench for Two' (1989) and the 'Trinidad' chair (1993). Throughout her life she exhibited internationally and won many awards.

RIGHT Nanna Ditzel's home, showing a pair of 'Trinidad' chairs, which she designed in 1993, in the foreground.

Nanna Ditzel

HANGING CHAIR (1957)
MANUFACTURER: Originally for Wengler of Amagertorv, Copenhagen
SPECIFICATION: Coated steel frame and chain suspension; woven rattan; drop in cotton seat.

This egg-shaped chair, also sometimes known as the 'Hammock' chair, was part of a range of wicker furniture designed by Nanna and Jørgen Ditzel for Wengler of Amagertorv, Copenhagen. The evocative elliptical form, expressed in tactile, homely wickerwork, represents a classic Scandinavian marriage of simplicity with organic sensibility.

RING CHAIR (1958) REISSUED AS SAUSAGE CHAIR (2007)
MANUFACTURER: Originally for Kold Savvaerk, Kerteminde; now produced by Artek
SPECIFICATION: Originally legs in laminated beech, maple or cherry; now legs in matt lacquered oak. Upholstered ring and seat covered in 'Hallingdal' fabric (black or red).

Like many Danish designs of the period, the Ditzels' version of an easy chair or armchair is a stunningly successful simplification of a traditional form and as such reflects the influence of Kaare Klint. The arms and back merge in one continuous padded ring set at exactly the right height to support the body. The seat is angled slightly towards the back, so that the sitter is naturally drawn into a relaxed posture. Tapering wooden legs extend upwards to support the upholstered ring, giving the design great clarity. The 'Ring' chair was reissued by Artek in 2005 and comes upholstered in Ditzel's phenomenally successful textile 'Hallingdal', which is still in production today.

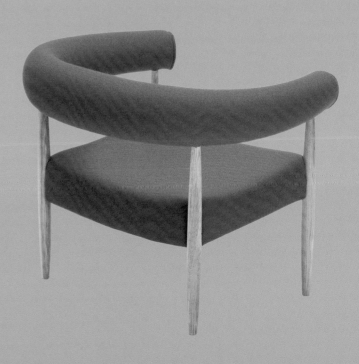

Tias Eckhoff

NORWEGIAN DESIGNER OF FLATWARE, TABLEWARE, GLASSWARE AND FURNITURE B.1926

Tias Eckhoff, Norway's most famous designer, made a significant contribution to Scandinavian modern. While a great deal of international attention was paid to products from Denmark, Sweden and Finland, Eckhoff's designs, many of which won awards and feature in museum collections, helped Norway retain a profile within the movement.

Eckhoff, an incredibly versatile designer, trained first in Denmark, where he was an apprentice at a pottery studio, then at the National College of Art and Design in Oslo, where he graduated in 1949. He began his career the same year, working as a designer for Porsgrund, a ceramics factory that was undergoing a programme of modernisation at the time. In 1952 his tea and coffee set 'The Fluted One' (Det Riflede) was a great success and from 1953 to 1960 he was artistic director of the company.

During the 1950s and 1960s, Eckhoff designed not only ceramics but glassware and metalware, including door furniture. It was his Cypress silver cutlery, designed in 1953 for Georg Jensen, that first brought him international recognition. Other flatware ranges, including 'Maya' (1961) were produced for Norsk Stalpress.

Later on, Eckhoff became interested in the potential of plastics and designed a number of chairs that featured injection-moulded seats. The recipient of numerous awards, at the age of 81 he was appointed Commander of the Royal Norwegian Order of St Olav in recognition of the significant contribution he has made to promoting Norwegian design.

DET RIFLEDE (THE FLUTED ONE) (1952)
MANUFACTURER Porsgrund
SPECIFICATION Tea and coffee set in white porcelain.

Eckhoff is committed to simplicity and functionalism, but never at the expense of beauty, and this service demonstrates his success at arriving at a perfectly judged solution. The refinement of form is matched by an understated tactility in the gentle rippled texture.

MAYA FLATWARE (1961)
MANUFACTURER Norsk Stalpress
SPECIFICATION Stainless steel flatware range.

Eckhoff proved equally adept at designing in metal as in ceramics. He produced a number of different flatware designs for Norsk Stalpress, but the best-known internationally is 'Maya'. Whether knife, fork or spoon, each piece seems to be reduced to an essential pure shape. Like much of Scandinavian modern, the cutlery invites you to use it and while the design is strongly contemporary, traditional form is not abandoned.

ABOVE AND BELOW
'Det Riflede' tea and coffee set.

Kaj Franck

RIGHT Brightly coloured mugs from the 'Teema' range.

FINNISH DESIGNER
(1911–89)

'An object must survive upon its own conditions instead of the designer's name, and design is an important part of those conditions.' FROM AN ARTICLE WRITTEN BY KAJ FRANCK IN 1966

Often called 'the conscience of Finnish design' Kaj Franck is best-known for his ceramics and glassware, although he also designed textiles and exhibitions. His work displays a characteristic Scandinavian duality – throughout his career he created highly individual one-off art or decorative pieces alongside utility ranges that promoted his notion of the importance of anonymity.

Franck trained as an interior architect and graduated from Helsinki's Institute of Technology in 1932. Up until the war, he worked as a window-dresser, interior designer and textile designer. In 1940 he had a brief stint working at Artek, where he designed two of their most popular fabrics, 'Putkinotko' and 'Lemon'.

After the upheaval of the war, Franck went to work for Arabia, a Finnish ceramics manufacturer located in Helsinki. During the 1930s Arabia had begun to develop utility designs for the mass market, a direction that would later flower in the postwar years under the banner of Scandinavian modern. A key figure in this endeavour was Kurt Ekholm (1907–1975), a Swedish-trained designer who founded Arabia's art department in 1932. Ekholm was influenced by the Funkis movement and was determined that good design should be within reach of everyone. His 'Sinivalko' (White-Blue) range, simple white stackable tableware banded in blue, which he designed for Arabia in 1936, bears certain similarities to Wilhelm Kåge's 'Praktika' service.

When Franck joined Arabia he was firmly convinced that design could be an agent of social change. As director of the design and

planning studio from 1946 to 1961, he was the driving force behind a whole new approach to tableware – designs that were inexpensive, attractive, and which could be used as table settings, for serving and for cooking. This multi-functional approach is epitomised by his 'Kilta' range (1952) and it was so revolutionary that part of the work of the studio was informing consumers about the benefits it delivered. Instead of using different dishes for entertaining and every day, or for cooking and serving, here was a range that met all these functions in one attractive package. The Kilta range, made of heat-resistant earthenware, was available in a family of plain colours; forms were simplified to the point where certain items could be used interchangeably; and pieces were marketed individually so that customers did not have to buy a complete service.

During the 1950s Arabia's products became widely known. Under Franck's direction many of the company's designers won prizes and international acclaim, specifically at the Milan Triennales in 1951, 1954 and 1957.

Franck also designed for the Nuutajärvi glassworks from 1950 to 1976, for almost all of that time serving as the company's artistic director. This followed a short period of association with Iittala, for whom he designed his famous 'Kartio' range of jugs and glasses.

Throughout his career Franck's work was shown widely in international exhibitions and received many prizes. He was also a highly influential design theorist and teacher.

TEEMA TABLEWARE (1977–80) BASED ON THE KILTA RANGE (1952)
MANUFACTURER: Arabia
SPECIFICATION: Ceramic range of tableware glazed in subtle colours; 19 separate pieces.

One of Franck's last design projects was to re-design his earlier 'Kilta' range so that it could be re-issued by Arabia. The 'Kilta' range demonstrated Franck's stated aim to 'smash the services', that is to break with the tradition of producing and marketing complete dinner services, which often put such wares out of the financial reach of ordinary families. 'Kilta', like its successor, 'Teema', was conceived as a series of separate pieces that could be bought according to need and means, and easily replaced.

The range reflects Franck's preoccupation both with simple geometric forms (circle, square and cone) and basic practicality. He shunned handles and other extraneous details, making the pieces more versatile, and did away with the broad decorative rims on plates so they could be stacked more easily. The palette of soft colours chosen for the glazing was inspired by the colours of the Finnish landscape.

KARTIO GLASSWARE (1958)
MANUFACTURER: Iittala
SPECIFICATION: Range of glassware available in a number of colours; tumblers, pitchers, vases.

Now half a century old, the 'Kartio' range of glassware is a classic example of Franck's dedication to the purity of form. The term 'kartio' means 'cone' in Finnish. By paring everyday objects down to their essentials, he ensured his designs had a timeless quality.

Franck was also an outstanding colourist and spent some time during the 1950s in Italy studying how glass pigments were made. While his art pieces were often vibrantly coloured, his utility ware was in subtler shades to allow food and drink to take centre stage.

Poul Henningsen

DANISH ARCHITECT, AND LIGHTING AND FURNITURE DESIGNER (1894–1967)

Born in Ordrup, a small Danish town, Poul Henningsen trained as an architect at the Technical School and the Danish College of Technology in Copenhagen. In 1920 he set up in practice, and subsequently designed several houses, a factory, part of Tivoli Gardens and two theatre interiors. He was also a committed socialist, outspoken reviewer and the editor, with Kaare Klint, of the architectural magazine *Kritisk Revy* (Critical Review).

From the age of 18, Henningsen had been interested in lighting, specifically how to recreate the soft gas-lit interiors of his youth using electrical light sources. As many others observed at the time, he saw how badly the then-new electrical lightbulb was being used, both in the home and public spaces. In the very early days of the technology, when electric lighting was a status symbol, it was not uncommon for bulbs to be suspended unshaded. Although these early bulbs were relatively low in wattage, it did not take long before the problem of glare arose. The 'dismal' interiors Henningsen saw from his tram were the result of people using lightbulbs as a direct substitution for gas lighting without considering how to temper the much higher level of illumination they provided. Henningsen wrote that the new technology 'gave the possibility of wallowing in light', stripping interiors of any sense of harmony and warmth.

Well before Henningsen set up his architectural practice, he began experimenting with lighting design, using different materials and approaching the subject scientifically, studying light diffusion and angles of reflection. From this period of research came the revolutionary series of PH lights in the mid 1920s. The first design in the series won all the prizes in a Danish lighting competition in 1924 and a gold medal in 1925, when it was exhibited in the Danish Pavilion at the Exposition Internationale des Arts Decoratifs in Paris.

The 'PH' series, a range of table and hanging lights, based on the same principles as the first so-called 'Paris' lamp, was almost immediately put into production by Louis Poulsen, the Danish lighting manufacturer, and they have remained in production, with a number of small modifications, ever since. The original fittings were produced in opal glass and were intended to be used in the home, although they were first adopted in commercial and public buildings. What is unique about the fittings is that they are composed of separate 'leaves' or elements, carefully positioned to diffuse light and reduce glare. Instead of a single bright concentrated source of light, setting up harsh contrasts, the overlapping planes create a much more comfortable ambient light.

The 'PH' series went on to become a huge critical and popular success, both in Scandinavia and internationally. Henningsen continued to design for Louis Poulsen. Another iconic fitting, the 'Artichoke' pendant lamp, dates from 1958.

RIGHT The 'Artichoke' pendant lamp makes a stunning focal point, its polished leaves gently diffusing the light.

Poul Henningsen

PH 5 (1958)

MANUFACTURER: Louis Poulsen
SPECIFICATION: Pendant light fitting, produced in aluminium. Available in either a grey or white painted finish.

A Danish design classic, and one that remains incredibly popular to this day, the PH 5 pendant is designed to hang low over a table. It is completely glare-free. All of Henningsen's lighting designs were the product of intensive research into the diffusion of light. The PH 5, so-called because the diameter of the topmost shade is 50cm, consists of three shades or reflectors that direct light both vertically and horizontally, a cone and two smaller coloured shades. The small red and blue shades are designed to correct the colour rendering of incandescent light sources. This design represents a considerable refinement on earlier PH fittings, as it remains completely glare-free no matter which type of bulb is used.

'It has always been the idea that the PH-lamp should be the lamp for the home. Due to its qualities and its modern appearance it had to be accepted first in offices and public buildings, but it is constructed with the most difficult and noble task in mind: lighting in the home. The aim is to beautify the home and those who live there, to make the evening restful and relaxing.' POUL HENNINGSEN

Poul Henningsen

PH ARTICHOKE LIGHT (1958)
MANUFACTURER: Louis Poulsen
SPECIFICATION: Available in copper or stainless steel, painted white and in three different sizes.

Originally conceived for Langelinie Pavilion, a restaurant in Copenhagen (where the lights are still hanging today), the 'Artichoke' is a completely glare-free pendant light designed so that it is impossible to see the light source from any direction. The light consists of 72 'leaves' mounted on 12 steel arches. The leaves or blades are arranged in 12 circular rows, with six leaves in each and the rows are staggered, giving rise to an organic form reminiscent of an artichoke, or, as in the original Danish name, a pine cone. Intended to be displayed in larger interiors, the pendant has great presence; it is also heavy and is consequently suspended by steel cable.

'When, in the evening, from the top of a tram car, you look into all the homes on the first floor, you shudder at how dismal people's homes are. Furniture, style, carpets, everything in the home is unimportant compared to the positioning of the lighting. It doesn't cost money to light a room correctly, but it does require culture.' POUL HENNINGSEN

Knud Holscher

DANISH ARCHITECT AND INDUSTRIAL DESIGNER B. 1930

'Design should be like buttons on a shirt. With character to catch your attention, but no more so than you can use it without thinking about it.' KNUD HOLSCHER, 2003

One of Denmark's leading architects, responsible for many public and private buildings in his native country, Knud Holscher is best-known internationally as an industrial designer, most particularly for his d-line range of architectural hardware. Holscher trained as an architect, studying under Arne Jacobsen at the Royal Danish Academy of Fine Arts, and graduated in 1957.

In the early 1960s Holscher worked for Arne Jacobsen in his architectural office, where he became an associate responsible for overseeing the construction of St Catherine's College, Oxford. During this period he came in contact with British designer Alan Tye (b. 1933), who was also employed by Jacobsen's office, and the two set up a design partnership together in Copenhagen in 1964. The result of that collaboration was the 'Modric' range of architectural hardware, which won a British Design Award in 1965.

In 1967 Holscher became a partner in the established Danish architectural firm Krohn & Hartvig Rasmussen, retiring in 1995 to head his own office Knud Holscher Design. Numerous public and private commissions have included the Royal Danish Theatre in Copenhagen (1978) and Copenhagen Airport (1983).

However, it is as an industrial designer that Holscher has made the greatest impact. His 'd-line' range of architectural hardware, designed in 1972, has won many awards and achieved huge international success. His practice has also been responsible for a wide range of other award-winning designs, including street furniture and signage.

D-LINE, ARCHITECTURAL HARDWARE (1972)
MANUFACTURER: Originally Carl F; now produced by d-line International
SPECIFICATION: Range of architectural hardware and sanitary fittings made of satin stainless steel.

Few contemporary architects are unfamiliar with the 'd-line' range of ironmongery and many around the world have specified such fittings in their buildings and interiors. The range began with a U-shaped lever handle, subsequently followed by an L-shaped lever handle. It now comprises 3,000 separate fittings and fixtures united by the same design concept.

Holscher's interest in architectural hardware began when he was acting as supervising architect on St Catherine's College, Oxford. Jacobsen's approach to this building was famously integrated, with many of the fixtures and fittings designed by his office. Holscher recalls having to search through many different brochures to come up with a coordinated ironmongery scheme: such ranges did not exist in the early 1960s.

After Holscher won an architectural competition to design a university in Odense, he was approached by Rolf Petersen, the proprietor of the tool manufacturer Carl F, and asked to develop a series of high quality fittings in stainless steel. A recent technical innovation that allowed steel tubes to be bent very precisely had prompted the proposal.

The 'd-line' range that resulted from this commission has become a contemporary classic of humane modernism. The fittings have the same radius throughout, which gives them a quality of balance and poise. The range has won many international awards.

PETER HVIDT
DANISH FURNITURE DESIGNER (1916–86)

ORLA MØLGAARD-NIELSEN
DANISH FURNITURE DESIGNER (1907–93)

The collaboration between these two cabinet-makers and designers, who worked in partnership between 1944 and 1975, resulted in a number of furniture designs that epitomised the Scandinavian modern aesthetic, particularly its Danish variant. Both men had backgrounds in cabinet-making and studied at the School of Arts and Crafts in Copenhagen. Mølgaard-Nielsen also trained under Kaare Klint, who impressed upon his students the need to relate furniture design to human measurements and postures. The work of Hvidt and Mølgaard-Nielsen similarly showed the influence of Klint's philosophy of updating traditional forms.

An early success was the 'Portex' chair (1944), an ingenious stacking chair in teak and intended for mass production. Their breakthrough, however, came when they began working with the Danish furniture manufacturer Fritz Hansen, which was then employing the technique of laminate-gluing, the same mode of construction used to make tennis rackets, and one that allowed rapid production without compromising quality.

Their most iconic work was the 'AX' chair they designed for Fritz Hansen (1947–50), which was accompanied by a series of 'AX' tables. But they also designed for other manufacturers, including France & Son and Søborg Møbelfabrik, producing many refined pieces, mostly in teak, which expressed the contemporary elegance of Scandinavian modern. Many of these have a sculptural quality that displays the influence of Finn Juhl.

AX CHAIR (1950)
MANUFACTURER: Fritz Hansen
SPECIFICATION: Chair in several variations; seat and back made of double curved laminated beechwood; accompanying series of AX tables.

The 'AX' chair, designed in 1947 and modified in 1950, was the undoubted highlight of Hvidt and Mølgaard-Nielsen's joint career. Inspired in part by the work of Charles and Ray Eames, the 'AX' became one of the best-selling chairs in Scandinavia during the 1950s, won many awards and was widely exhibited, notably at the 1951 'Good Design' show sponsored by MoMA. Because it was designed so that the seat and back could be dismantled and packaged separately, the product was easily shipped for the export trade. The 'AX' chair came in several variations and was accompanied by a number of different 'AX' tables.

Like much of their work, the design of these pieces does not represent any type of radical departure, but a subtle updating of traditional forms combined with technical innovation. Exceptionally pleasing on the eye, comfortable, and of high quality, the 'AX' chair argued persuasively in favour of the supreme liveability of Danish design.

Peter Hvidt &
Orla Mølgaard-Nielsen

Maija Isola

FINNISH TEXTILE DESIGNER AND ARTIST (1927–2001)

'I had a huge floral still-life of sorts spread out wet on the floor, waiting to be rolled up…paints in yoghurt pots, and newspaper everywhere, and flowers in vases on the floorboards…Large deep-red roses, small and fragrant, curiously furry pink ones, yellow, orange and white poppies, cowslips in various shades of purple, black tulips and tiny carmine flowers whose name I don't know.'
MAIJA ISOLA, WRITING TO HER DAUGHTER FROM PARIS, 1970

Throughout her long association with the well-known Finnish textile company Marimekko, Maija Isola produced many of the company's most popular designs. Examples of her work can still be seen widely today, cropping up in a host of applications – from bedlinen and shower curtains to rubber boots and walking sticks. Her bold flower print 'Unikko' (Poppy), first designed in 1964, has seen a huge revival in recent years and has now become something of a Marimekko trademark.

Maija Isola studied textiles at the Central School of Arts and Crafts (now known as the University of Art and Design) in Helsinki, graduating in 1949. Her first printed textiles were designed for Printex, a textile company founded the same year. At that time, clothing was in short supply in Finland and the new company was set up to address the need. Isola designed a number of striking screen-printed cotton fabrics for the company before going to work for its subsidiary, Marimekko, which was founded in 1951 to promote Printex fabrics through collections of interior furnishings and clothing.

Many of Isola's best-known designs date from the 1960s, a time that saw Marimekko become established internationally. Throughout the 1950s, the company had struggled, but after it exhibited at the 1958 World's Fair in Brussels, international orders, particularly from the United States, set it on a firm footing.

As both an artist and textile designer, Isola took inspiration from a wide variety of sources, including folk art, modern art, nature and the many different countries she visited around the world. Many of the sketches and paintings she made on her travels were later used as a basis for prints. Her crisp graphic style and use of strong flat colour were hugely influential and her body of work, which includes over 500 prints, 50 of which are in current production, has remained remarkably enduring.

ABOVE The original 'Unikko' design, from 1964.

BELOW The Keiju cosmetics bag and 'Mini-Unikko' tray, a small-scale version of the original 'Unikko' design, are modern-day applications.

Maija Isola

UNIKKO (POPPY) (1964)
MANUFACTURER: Marimekko
SPECIFICATION: Printed cotton fabric, available in a wide range of colours and different scales; design is also produced in Teflon-coated cotton.

Isola was always interested in nature, and early natural prints in the 1950s were produced using a type of photogram process, where real plants were used to create the pattern. At the same time she was also designing in a bold geometric style. With 'Unikko', these two directions joined forces and the result would become the most popular of all Marimekko textiles.

When Printex, Marimekko's parent company, was first set up, its founders Viljo Ratia and his wife Armi were determined to find a new direction for textile design. Much of what was available in the immediate post-war years were insipid floral prints. After Armi Ratia publicly announced in 1964 that no floral fabrics were produced by Marimekko, Isola saw this as a challenge and came up with this bright poppy print, which ironically has now virtually become the company's trademark.

A huge number of different products are now available in this design. Isola's daughter, Kristina, has come up with a 'Mini-Unikko' range for children and has also introduced new colourways.

Maija Isola

LOKKI (SEAGULL) (1961)
MANUFACTURER: Marimekko
SPECIFICATION: Printed textile in 100% cotton;
available in three colours; 113cm repeat.

This classic graphic print by Isola dates from the
early 1960s and is one of a number of large-
scale designs she produced during this time.

KAIVO (WELL) (1964)
MANUFACTURER: Marimekko
SPECIFICATION: Printed textile in 100% cotton; available in several colourways; 86cm repeat.

The graphic punch of 'Kaivo' owes something to Isola's fascination with African tribal art. Kristina Isola, Maija's daughter, has introduced a number of new colourways for the patterns her mother created in the 1960s.

Maija Isola

Arne Jacobsen

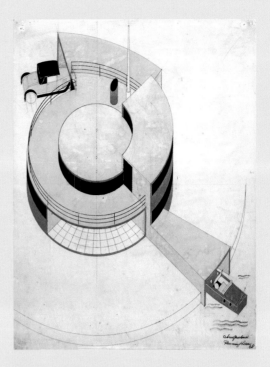

RIGHT 'House of the Future', an early
concept house designed by Jacobsen
and Flemming Lassen in 1929.

DANISH ARCHITECT AND DESIGNER
(1902–71)

'…the buildings one enjoys looking at, those
one admires, are all well-proportioned, that is
absolutely essential. Next comes the material
– not mixing the wrong materials. And out of
this comes, of course, the colour – and, in
sum, the overall impression.' ARNE JACOBSEN

Arne Jacobsen is arguably the leading figure of
Scandinavian modern design, rivalled only by
Alvar Aalto in international fame and success.
A prolific and versatile designer, who could turn
his attention to anything from the design of a
national bank to the small round pull at the end
of a roller blind, he was also responsible for a
number of landmark buildings both in his native
country and abroad.

Jacobsen was born in Copenhagen. His
father was a wholesale trader in safety pins and
fasteners; his mother a bank clerk and amateur
painter. The family was of Portuguese Jewish
descent. His parents, who were relatively
elderly, decided to send their lively son to
boarding school, where he met Flemming
Lassen, who would later collaborate with him on
a number of building projects.

As a schoolboy Jacobsen was already
demonstrating a strong visual bent. Inspired by
early modernists such as Mies van der Rohe and
Le Corbusier, he painted his bedroom at home
white, obliterating the busy wallpaper, much to
his parents' dismay. He excelled at drawing,
particularly studies of nature, and originally
wanted to become an artist, until his father
persuaded him that architecture was a more
sensible choice.

Like many great Scandinavian designers,
Jacobsen had a background both in practical
and artistic disciplines. He first trained to be a
mason at the School of Applied Arts in
Copenhagen and then studied architecture at the
Royal Danish Academy of Fine Arts, graduating
in 1927. During his student days he travelled

widely and kept up with international trends in
design. Gunnar Asplund was a particular hero,
from whom he absorbed the lesson that good
design relies as much on hard work as it does
on talent.

Two years after graduation Jacobsen co-
designed an exhibition house with Flemming
Lassen. 'The House of the Future' was a modernist
essay, a circular house in white concrete featuring
a helipad on the roof and a vacuum cleaner built
into the doormat that buzzed as it removed the
dust from people's shoes.

His first major commission, however, came
in 1932 when he designed an entertainment
complex at Bellevue, a popular seaside resort.
Here Jacobsen already displayed the integrated
approach to design that would become such a
strong feature of his later work. At Bellevue he
was responsible not only for the Bellavista
apartment block and Bellevue theatre, but also
the design of interiors, furniture, lifeguard towers,
ice cream packaging and tickets. The theatre
auditorium has a curving bamboo-clad balcony
and undulating rows of bent ply seats.

In 1936 Jacobsen set up in partnership with
Erik Møller after they won a competition to
design Arhus Town Hall (1942). While the early
projects in which Jacobsen revealed his debt to
Corbusier earned him some hostility from the
Danish public, who were markedly traditional in
their tastes and conservative in outlook, this
significant commission saw him adopt a more
humanistic approach, particularly in the

treatment of interior spaces and furnishing. The interior featured wood panelled walls and rounded detailing.

During the war Jacobsen was one of the Danish Jews who had to flee into exile in Sweden. In 1943 he and his second wife Jonna, along with Poul Henningsen and his wife, made the four-hour sea crossing to safety in a rowboat.

For the rest of the war, Jacobsen turned his attention to textile designs, collaborating with Jonna, who was a printer. Patterns from this period were stylised natural motifs, reflecting Jacobsen's deep interest in plants and plant forms. Later, in his own garden, he grew 300 different species, with clipped walls of hedges setting up outdoor rooms defined by different surfaces, textures and shapes. Textile design remained a preoccupation throughout the remainder of his career, although natural forms eventually gave way to Op-Art inspired geometric designs.

Return to Denmark after the war saw Jacobsen design one of the country's first modern schools, Munkegaard School, in 1957.

The blocky 'Series 3300' sofa and chair, which are still in production, were conceived for this school, along with desks, school chairs in various sizes and a host of other details and features, from drinking fountains to stage curtains.

Jacobsen rarely, if ever, designed furniture and fittings out of a specific context. During the 1950s and 1960s he had outstanding international success with his 'Ant' series of chairs (1951–2), originally designed for the Novo canteen, and the 'Series 7' chair, one of the most popular and iconic chairs ever put into mass production, which was designed for Rødovre town hall. The 'AJ' lamp also dates from this period and made its first appearance in a wall-mounted bracket version at the SAS check-in lounge.

With the SAS Royal Hotel in Copenhagen (1960) Jacobsen's reputation as a leading architect and designer was sealed. Again, local critics found his interpretation of the International Style confounding, likening the rectilinear form of the building, with its gridded elevation, to a 'punchcard' or a 'glass cigar box'. Inside, the straight lines and pure geometries are softened

ABOVE Two early Jacobsen textile designs, reflecting his deep interest in nature.

Arne Jacobsen

by the curvaceous forms of the furniture, glassware and cutlery, a soothing palette of blue-greens, and an internal orchid garden that serves as a light shaft. At the SAS Royal Hotel, every interior detail was designed by Jacobsen, from lighting to textiles, ashtrays to cutlery. The result is a remarkable unity of organic forms and functional integrity.

The 'Egg' and the 'Swan' chairs, the most famous and enduring furniture designs associated with this scheme, were first launched by Jacobsen in Paris. This was a marketing ploy intended to ensure that their subsequent visibility as Danish designs would persuade his SAS clients, who had not yet asked him to design any furniture, to select the pieces for the hotel interiors, which they duly did.

Jacobsen's last major completed work was also his only significant building outside Denmark. This was St Catherine's College, Oxford (1964), his modernist interpretation of the traditional Oxbridge college with its enclosed quadrangle. One of the reasons why he was selected to design the new college, according to Lord Bullock, then the college's founding Master, was because of the sensitivity he had shown at Munkegaard School, where details and furniture were carefully scaled down so that children could comfortably use them. Of the many details, fittings, fixtures and furniture Jacobsen created specifically for St Catherine's, only the Oxford series of high-backed chairs are still in production.

When Jacobsen died he left incomplete a number of commissions, including the Danish National Bank in Copenhagen, now regarded as a landmark building. The Vola bathroom fittings he designed in 1969 for this scheme are still produced today.

As Professor at the Royal Danish Academy for eleven years, Jacobsen influenced a whole generation of Danish architects. He also won numerous prestigious awards. His failure to make an impact in the United States as an architect, or to win any commissions there, has

been ascribed to his fear of flying. He also suffered badly from seasickness and his only journey to America, when he sailed to New York as a young man, was not repeated.

Today, in both architecture and product design, Jacobsen's legacy is assured. A legendary perfectionist, he pushed technology and materials to their limit, sometimes without being altogether sure at the outset that what he had conceived was physically possible. With clients, staff and manufacturers he could be difficult, obsessive and dictatorial, expecting others to put in the same hours and effort that he did. At the same time, he had a jovial, funny side and was an ardent botanist who delighted in living organic forms. That combination of rigour and modernity, with an instinctive, soulful appreciation of nature is the essence of the Scandinavian modern approach.

'[The architect] must build his houses as honestly and as aesthetically correct as possible – so there is hope that the people who are going to live in them can learn to see what is ugly and what is beautiful and in time throw the ugly things out.' ARNE JACOBSEN

SWAN CHAIR (1958)

MANUFACTURE: Fritz Hansen

SPECIFICATION: Seat shell made of moulded fibreglass, foam-covered and upholstered; swivelling star base in aluminium. Upholstered in fabric or leather. Also available in a sofa version.

The 'Swan' chair was designed at the same time as the 'Egg', also for the SAS Royal Hotel in Copenhagen. A sofa version, which featured in the original interiors, has recently been put back into production.

Like the 'Egg', the chair is an essay in curves. Its organic form, with uplifted arms or wings, is even more suggestive of the bird after which it is named when a number of chairs are gathered together. Viewed from above, the chair also resembles an orchid. The internal glass-screened garden at the hotel featured over 30 species of the flower.

ABOVE The sofa version of the 'Swan' chair.

Arne Jacobsen

RIGHT The 'Ant' chair is available today in a huge range of colours.

ANT CHAIR, MODEL 3100 (1951-2)

MANUFACTURER: Fritz Hansen

SPECIFICATION: Series of chairs with back and seat made of a single shell of laminated wood (nine layers of moulded veneer with two layers of cotton textile sandwiched in between). Available in three- or four-legged versions; legs in chromed or satin chromed steel. Huge range of colours, or in beech or dark-stained oak finishes.

Jacobsen designed the 'Ant' chair for one of his architectural schemes, the Novo canteen. A key feature of the design was the fact that it had three legs, which made it stackable. Although a four-legged 'Ant' chair is also available today (Model 3101), it was only put into production after Jacobsen's death, as he considered the three-legged version to be the only acceptable one.

Jacobsen approached the Danish manufacturer Fritz Hansen, the leading exponents of pressure moulding techniques, to put the chair into mass production. He had no objection to realising his designs in plastic, but manufacturing in plastic requires expensive machinery that Danish furniture companies at that time could not justify, given the size of their local market. To achieve the right curves, Jacobsen modelled the design first in clay, going through some ten prototypes before he was satisfied the chair was ready for manufacture. 'I have tormented the elasticity of the wood to the extreme,' he said.

The design was based on the need for an inexpensive, stackable space-saving chair that would suit both public spaces, such as canteens and lecture halls, and private homes. When the 'Ant' was launched in 1952 it was not an immediate success, but it has since become one of Jacobsen's most distinctive and enduring designs. The back profile, which clearly reflects the chair's name, is instantly recognisable.

'The first chair took me a year to make before I dared to let it out. A large and costly apparatus is put in motion when a chair is to be manufactured serially. I myself stood and modelled it to achieve the right curves, which are decisive for the seating position. We cannot see the cut, but we feel it. It is right if we rest in it. Then we can make the chair's appearance correspond to our view of what looks good.'

ARNE JACOBSEN, ON THE 'ANT'

Arne Jacobsen

RIGHT Room 606 at the SAS Royal Hotel, Copenhagen, showing 'Egg' and 'Swan' chairs, as well as the 'Series 3300' sofa and armchairs, originally designed for the Munkegaard School. This is the only hotel room with the original Jacobsen designed décor dating from July 1960.

EGG CHAIR (1958) MODEL NO. 3316
MANUFACTURER: Fritz Hansen
SPECIFICATION: Moulded fibreglass shell, padded with foam and covered in fabric, vinyl or leather. Star-shaped cast aluminium swivel base. Can be adjusted or tilted to accommodate the sitter's weight. Available with accompanying footstool. Separate seat cushion.

Designed for the lobby and reception areas of the SAS Royal Hotel, Copenhagen, the 'Egg' chair is an icon of Danish design and has never been out of production. At the Royal Hotel, there was also a sofa version of the 'Egg' but it was never put into mass production.

The prototype for the 'Egg' chair was cast in plaster in the designer's garage. A streamlined, abstracted version of the classic wingchair, it provides a comfortable sense of enclosure: you fill the space with your body. The smooth curves were intended to serve as a foil for the clean lines of Jacobsen's interiors and the design is as effective a spatial marker as it is clustered in seating groups.

The chair is demanding to produce, as the upholstery must fit perfectly so as not to detract from the pure organic form. It is available covered either in leather, vinyl or in fabric dyed strong clear colours. Lately, designers such as Paul Smith and Tord Boontje have given this contemporary classic a new twist and a note of irreverence by creating patterned fabric for the upholstery.

RIGHT Transformation of a design icon: Tord Boontje's contemporary floral fabric used to upholster an Egg chair.

'As thin as possible and never in the middle.'
ARNE JACOBSEN ON MINIMALISM

Designed in 1955 as a variation on the 'Ant' series, the 'Model 3107' chair rapidly evolved into a series of its own, 'Series 7'. It received a much more favourable reception at its launch: critics liked the fact that the chair had four legs and there was the option of arms. Since then, the chair has become the most commercially successful design of all time, selling 5 million copies to date.

The original chair was available in a number of wood veneers, including teak. A range of eight bright colours, designed by Jacobsen, was added in 1968; this colour range was extended by Verner Panton in 1972 and now comprises 30 different shades.

The rounded triangular back and seat, linked by an obvious waist, is suggestive of the female form, an association strengthened by the infamous photograph of Christine Keeler, apparently seated astride it. The real story was somewhat different, as Keeler was actually posing on a knock-off version of the design. Lewis Morley, the photographer who took the pictures, had bought six of the chairs in 1960 when they were on sale at Heals for five shillings each. The slot cut out of the back, which does not feature on any Jacobsen design, was the manufacturers' way of avoiding a suit for breach of copyright.

SERIES 7, MODEL 3107 (1955)
MANUFACTURER: Fritz Hansen
SPECIFICATION: Series of chairs, with seat and back made of a single slim shell (nine layers of beechwood veneer, sandwiched with two layers of cotton textile); optional arms; base of mirror-chromed or satin-chromed steel. Variations include: side chair, pedestal chair, office chair, bar stool, counter chair and a small children's version. Huge range of colours; finishes include lacquer, painted beech, coloured ash and wood veneer. Leather or fabric upholstered versions also available.

TOWN HALL CLOCK (1955)
MANUFACTURER: Originally produced by Louis Poulsen, subsequently by Georg Christensen. Re-edition available from Romer, Germany
SPECIFICATION: Glass and chromium plated steel ring. Re-edition features aluminium ring and quartz movement; available in two sizes.

Jacobsen designed a number of clocks during his career, most often for specific locations. This design was created for Rødovre Town Hall. A classic modern design, the face is a model of clarity, the clock hands and hour marks finely judged in proportion.

RIGHT Jacobsen designed a number of clocks. The 'Town Hall' clock is on the near left.

Arne Jacobsen

AJ (VISOR) FLOOR LAMP (1957)
MANUFACTURER: Louis Poulsen
SPECIFICATION: Aluminium shade with metal pipe stand and cast-iron base; available in wall-mounted and table versions; black, grey or white painted finish.

The 'AJ' lamp made its first appearance as a wall-mounted fitting in the SAS departure lounge. Later the design was developed both as a table and floor-standing lamp. The cone-shaped shade, which can be tilted, is enamelled matt white inside, and directs the light precisely. When the lamp is angled downwards, the edge of the shade is horizontal. At all times the light source cannot be seen, shielded by the steep visor-like angle of the metal shade. The asymmetry of the design and its eager forward tilt animate it with personality. According to rumour, the circular cut-out in the base was originally intended to accommodate an ashtray.

AJ ROYAL PENDANT (1957)
MANUFACTURER: Louis Poulsen
SPECIFICATION: Spun aluminium shade with steel rings; white painted finish.

Jacobsen had a keen interest in the design of light fittings and was a close friend of the celebrated Danish lighting designer Poul Henningsen. Like Henningsen, Jacobsen often deplored the quality of light in public spaces. This pendant fixture, designed for the SAS Royal Hotel, conceals the light source within its hemispherical shade. Soft uplight is emitted through the stepped ring louvres at the top.

VOLA TAP AND BATHROOM FITTINGS (1969)
MANUFACTURER: Vola
SPECIFICATION: Range of taps and bathroom fittings in chrome and brass.

In 1961, after Jacobsen won a competition to design the Danish National Bank he was contacted by Verner Overgaard, the owner of Vola, who proposed a new concept for a mixer tap where all the mechanical parts were hidden. The simplicity and functionalism of the idea appealed to Jacobsen and the result was an entirely new type of tap, where the spout emerged from the wall as if it were a continuation of a water pipe. Since Jacobsen's death, many new products have been introduced into the Vola range.

AJ CUTLERY (1957)
MANUFACTURER: Georg Jensen
SPECIFICATION: Matt or polished stainless steel.

The original flatware range, designed for the SAS Royal Hotel, consisted of 21 separate pieces: teaspoons, knives and forks of different sizes, a pastry knife and soup spoons for right- and left-handed use. Early drawings show a more organic quality to the forms but what eventually went into production was so minimalist, sculptural and innovative that the cutlery featured a decade later in Stanley Kubrick's *2001: A Space Odyssey*. It remains just as bold and radical looking today.

Like many of the smaller items – candleholders, ashtrays and so on – that Jacobsen designed for the hotel, the cutlery was not in use very long and was soon replaced with flatware that was less challenging for popular taste. Yet it has remained in continuous production since it was designed. The pieces sit well in the hand, allowing free movement.

CYLINDA-LINE HOLLOWWARE (1967)
MANUFACTURER: Stelton
SPECIFICATION: Tableware range including jugs, coffee pots, ice bucket, salad bowl, salt and pepper set, amongst others; stainless steel with Bakelite handles.

Three years in development, the 'Cylinda-Line' is a distinctive tableware range that resembles a contemporary urban skyline when displayed together. The uniting concept behind the design is the basic tubular shape, with spouts attached low down and angular grips for handles. At home Jacobsen used the ice bucket, which has insulated sides, as a soup tureen.

No less futuristic than Jacobsen's cutlery, the 'Cylinda-Line' has also found its way onto sci-fi filmsets. In *I, Robot* Will Smith can be seen pouring himself a cup of coffee from the 'Cylinda' coffee pot.

Finn Juhl

DANISH ARCHITECT AND DESIGNER
(1912–89)

'One cannot create happiness with beautiful objects, but one can spoil quite a lot of happiness with bad ones.' FINN JUHL

Although Finn Juhl is internationally renowned as a furniture designer, he initially trained as an architect. In furniture design, he was self-taught and began by producing furniture for his own use, as many architects before and since have done.

Juhl was born on the outskirts of Copenhagen. His father, who was rather authoritarian, was a textile wholesaler and his mother died soon after his birth. While he was still at school, he developed an early interest in art history and hoped to pursue a career in it, but his father persuaded him to enrol at the Royal Danish Academy of Fine Arts and study architecture. Juhl's introduction to functionalism was the seminal 1930 exhibition organised by Gunnar Asplund. At the Academy, he was also taught by another aficionado of the style, Kay Fisker, who was known for his inspired lectures and slide shows.

In 1934 Juhl went to work for Vilhelm Lauritzen, a practising architect who also taught at the Academy, and remained in the office for 11 years. It was during this time that he began to design furniture, working in collaboration with a master cabinet-maker Niels Vodder, an association that lasted until 1959. The 'Pelikan' chair, which dates from 1940, represented a radical break both from tradition and from the evolutionary approach promoted by Kaare Klint. 'Poeten', a design he produced for his own house the following year, displays the same sculptural abstract modelling of form.

After the war, Juhl set up his own design practice. Throughout the 1950s, he designed a number of private houses, exhibitions and shop interiors, as well as continuing to produce furniture, much of it exquisitely handmade

and displaying a refinement of teak jointing techniques that helped to make the tropical hardwood the signature of the new Danish modern style. His pieces were widely exhibited and he won many awards, including five gold medals at the Milan Triennales during the 1950s.

One particular exhibition, however, the 1951 'Good Design' show in Chicago, proved a turning point for Juhl and Danish modern design in general. Juhl designed an interior for the exhibition where his furniture was displayed and was immediately commissioned by Baker Furniture Inc., of Michigan, to develop a range of mass-produced furniture in the same contemporary style. The original range (1951–55) comprised 24 pieces, including chairs, tables, sideboards, desks and storage units.

In 1952 Juhl found further international recognition when he designed the Trusteeship Council Chamber at the UN Headquarters in New York and the interior of the Georg Jensen store on Fifth Avenue. Aside from furniture, interiors and exhibitions, he also turned his hand to a number of different disciplines throughout his long and productive career, designing ceramics and glassware, teak bowls for Kay Bojesen's workshop, as well as the DC-8 cabin for SAS. In 1978 Britain recognised his achievements when he was made Honorary Royal Designer for Industry.

Finn Juhl

PELIKAN CHAIR (1940)
MANUFACTURER: Originally hand-produced by Niels Vodder, now manufactured under licence by Hansen & Sorensen
SPECIFICATION: Easy chair with hand-sewn upholstery, separate seat cushion and wooden legs; also available in leather.

Designed by Juhl in 1940 for his own house, the 'Pelikan' chair is a very early indication of the direction Scandinavian modern design would take in the 1950s and 1960s. A radical interpretation of a wing chair, where the organic form of wings seem to invite you to sit within the chair's embrace, the design reflects the influence that modern artists such as Henry Moore, Picasso and Alexander Calder had upon Juhl's work at this time.

MODEL 45 EASY CHAIR (1945)
MANUFACTURER: Originally hand-produced by Niels Vodder, now manufactured under licence by Hansen & Sorensen
SPECIFICATION: Back and seat upholstered in leather; frame available in a number of woods.

One of Juhl's most iconic designs, the 'Model 45' shows the refinement that his work became famous for. This ground-breaking design freed the back and seat from the supporting frame and represented a significant departure at the time. The fluidity of the frame, which contributes so much to the elegance of the design, was made possible by developments in teak jointing techniques pioneered by Juhl. It was originally available in a number of dark woods, including rosewood, mahogany and walnut, as well as teak.

Finn Juhl

POETEN SOFA (1941)
MANUFACTURER: Originally hand-produced by Niels Vodder, now manufactured under licence by Hansen & Sorensen

SPECIFICATION: Small two-seater sofa with hand-sewn upholstery and wooden legs.

Another piece Juhl designed for his own home, 'Poeten' shows the same interest in abstract, sculptural form. Many Juhl designs, especially the mass-production range he produced for Baker Furniture Inc. in the 1950s were available only as vintage pieces until Hansen & Sorensen acquired the licence to put the furniture into production.

CHIEFTAIN CHAIR (1949)

MANUFACTURER: Originally hand-produced by Niels Vodder, now manufactured under licence by Hansen & Sorensen

SPECIFICATION: Leather upholstered back, seat and armrests; frame in teak or walnut.

One of the designs that made Juhl's name in the United States and helped launch the success of Danish modern, the 'Chieftain' chair displays Juhl's characteristic refinement, along with shapes borrowed from shields and armoury. Like many classic Scandinavian modern designs, the chair is animated with personality.

MODEL 57 SOFA (1957)

MANUFACTURER: Produced under licence by Hansen & Sorensen

SPECIFICATION: Upholstered sofa with hand-woven spring inserts; available in fabric or leather; legs in brushed stainless steel with wooden feet.

Originally designed for Tivoli, Copenhagen in 1957, this sofa was first put into production during the late 1990s by Hansen & Sorensen, reflecting the renewed upsurge of interest in mid-century modern.

Poul Kjaerholm

DANISH ARCHITECT AND FURNITURE DESIGNER (1929–80)

'I consider steel a material with the same artistic merit as wood and leather.'
POUL KJAERHOLM

Born in a small village in Jutland, Poul Kjaerholm was apprenticed to a local cabinetmaker at the age of 15. Once his apprenticeship was completed, he moved to Copenhagen and was admitted to the School of Arts and Crafts in 1949. Here he was taught by a number of influential Danish designers, including Hans Wegner; he also attended Kaare Klint's lectures and spent some time studying under Jørn Utzon, who would later become world famous as the architect of Sydney Opera House.

Unlike Wegner and Klint, who expressed their modernity in wood, right from the beginning of his career Kjaerholm was drawn to the possibilities offered by steel construction, greatly influenced in this respect by the work of Charles and Ray Eames and Mies van der Rohe. While Kjaerholm developed the basic concept for a chair in moulded plywood (nearly half a century later put into production as the 'PK0' chair) in the early 1950s, his graduation piece in 1952 was the elegantly minimal 'PK25' chair in steel with seat and back made of flag halyard. Kjaerholm had worked out the jointing techniques used in the chair's construction by experimenting in a local forge during his summer holidays.

Although Kjaerholm spent a year after his graduation working for Fritz Hansen, who put the 'PK25' chair into limited production, it was his association with the Danish furniture maker E. Kold Christensen, which began in 1955 and continued to his death, which saw the launch of his commercial career. The 'PK22' easy chair, put into production in 1956, set the seal on his international reputation and won the designer the prestigious Lunning Award in 1958.

Throughout his career, which was cut short by his early death, Kjaerholm pursued the quest for a rational, minimalist ideal. Unlike other Scandinavian designers, he largely expressed his concepts of form in steel, which he considered every bit as artistic a material as wood. However, by partnering steel frameworks with softer materials such as leather, rope and woven cane, he was able to create spare modernist designs that retain the human quality characteristic of Scandinavian modern. Highly articulate, Kjaerholm was an influential teacher, first as a lecturer at the Royal Danish Academy of Fine Arts and later as Professor at the Institute of Design. After his death, Fritz Hansen took over the production of his designs.

BELOW The 'PK22' chair, designed in 1955.

RIGHT Interior of the house designed by Hanne Kjaerholm in Rungsted, Denmark (1961). It provides a showcase for her husband's furniture.

PK24 CHAISE LONGUE, ALSO KNOWN AS THE HAMMOCK CHAISE (1965)
MANUFACTURER: E. Kold Christensen; later reissued by Fritz Hansen
SPECIFICATION: Stainless steel frame, seat and back either in woven cane or leather; adjustable leather headrest with steel counterweight. Leather upholstery available in different colours.

Perhaps Kjaerholm's most recognisable design, the 'PK24' chaise longue is supremely refined and clearly derives from the chaise longue designed in the 1920s by Le Corbusier and Charlotte Perriand. The curved seat and back glide on the steel frame so that the sitter can adjust their position: it has been described as a 'diagram of relaxation'. Until 2007, the chaise was always produced in woven cane; since then a leather version has been available. Even though Kjaerholm's designs were largely machine-made, the attention to detail they display and high standard of construction required to produce them result in an enduring sense of quality.

Poul Kjaerholm

PK80 DAYBED (1957)
MANUFACTURER: E. Kold Christensen;
later produced by Fritz Hansen
SPECIFICATION: Low bench consisting of
a mattress upholstered in leather supported
by painted ply and resting on a satin
brushed stainless steel base. Leather
upholstery available in a range of colours.

The 'PK80' daybed is an icon of minimalist
design and one of Kjaerholm's most
famous pieces. Its low height (30cm) is a
characteristic feature. For MoMA in New
York, where the daybed provides seating
in many of the museum's rooms, Fritz
Hansen produced a slightly higher version.

PK22 CHAIR (1955)
MANUFACTURER: E. Kold Christensen; later put
into production by Fritz Hansen
SPECIFICATION: Steel spring framework; seat
and back in leather or suede in four colours.
A version with a slightly higher back is also
available where the seat and back are made of
woven cane.

The 'PK22', Kjaerholm's elegant response to Mies
van der Rohe's classic Barcelona chair, came
directly out of the experiments into steel jointing
that he had been carrying out during the
development of the 'PK25' chair. Like many of
Kjaerholm's designs, the chair appears to be
simplicity itself, yet is the product of intense
research and attention to detail. Even joints that
are not visible are models of perfection.
    Kjaerholm's designs are demanding to
produce. His collaboration with his friend, Kold
Christensen, allowed him the artistic freedom he
required to pursue his ideals.

Yrjo Kukkapuro

FINNISH FURNITURE DESIGNER
B.1933

Yrjo Kukkapuro, one of Finland's most influential designers, is best known outside his native country for the 'Karuselli' (Carousel) chair (1964–5), which took the international design community by storm when it appeared on the front cover of *Domus* in 1966. It has since become emblematic of modern Finnish design.

Kukkapuro studied at the University of Art and Design in Helsinki. Here he was greatly influenced by the functionalist approach of Ilmari Tapiovaara, who taught there, a designer who spent much of his career trying to perfect a multipurpose chair and who had himself once worked as an apprentice in Le Corbusier's office in Paris.

Kukkapuro's early chair designs had moulded plywood seats and tubular steel frames, chiefly because these were the materials that were readily available in Finland. All the while, however, he was thinking about producing chairs in plastic and developed a couple of prototypes that proved too expensive to put into production – manufacturing in plastic required expensive machinery that Finland's producers could not support at the time.

His breakthrough came with the 'Karuselli' chair, which took a year of development. Its combination of functionalism with a soft moulded shape heralded a new direction in Finnish design. Other designs in moulded plastic followed until the oil crisis in the 1970s again ruled out the use of the material. In the late 1970s, Kukkapuro experimented with designs based on ergonomic principles and subsequently created a number of playful post-modernist pieces.

KARUSELLI (CAROUSEL) CHAIR (1965)
MANUFACTURER: Originally Haimi;
now produced by Avarte
SPECIFICATION: Swivelling and rocking
armchair, with seat shell and base made of
fibreglass; white or black leather upholstery;
chrome plated steel spring and rubber dampers
connecting seat to base; footstool available.

Kukkapuro had been interested in producing a
chair in moulded plastic for some time. Then one
winter day in 1964 he happened to be playing
in the snow with his daughter, Isa, making snow
chairs. He was so inspired by the results that he
hurried to his studio to see if he could reproduce
the effect in real materials. The prototype for the
'Karuselli' chair was made out of chicken wire,
shaped to fit his seated body and mounted on a

steel frame. Then the wire mesh was covered in
canvas dipped in plaster, which he modelled into
a form he was happy with, a process of
development that took nearly a year.

When the prototype was ready, Kukkapuro
took it the Helsinki furniture shop Haimi for
discussion and comment. During the meeting,
which took place early in the morning when the
shop was still closed, a customer wandered in
through a door that had been accidentally left
open, noticed the prototype, sat on it and
announced that he would take one.

'Karuselli' has since become a classic of
modern Finnish design, functional but organic in
form and the product of experimentation in
materials and technology. Kukkapuro's concern to
produce a comfortable chair that would echo the
form of the human body was a logical extension
of his interest in functionalism and prefigured his
later ergonomic work.

Yrjo Kukkapuro

Stig Lindberg

SWEDISH DESIGNER
(1916–82)

One of Sweden's most prolific and best-known designers, Stig Lindberg's work in ceramics, textiles and glassware exemplifies Scandinavian modern. Many of his pieces are still present in Swedish homes, while originals command high prices on the international collectors' market.

Between 1935 and 1937 Lindberg studied at the University College of Arts, Crafts and Design in Stockholm. His original intention was to be a painter. After graduation, he went to work as a faience painter at the Gustavsberg ceramics factory, training under Wilhelm Kåge, who was a great influence on him. He also studied for a time in Denmark and Paris.

There are two distinct strands to Lindberg's work. One is colourful and decorative, with figurative designs based on folk art, and the other is more organic and sculptural. A good example of the figurative side are the two textiles he designed in 1947 for an exhibition curated by Astrid Sampe, 'Lustgarden' (Garden of Eden) and 'Pottery'. His painted earthenware ranges and whimsical ceramic figures, designed for Gustavsberg, also fall into this category. During the 1950s his designs became more organic and sculptural, essays in pure form and often asymmetrical. While some of these ceramics were decorated, patterns were more abstract and in the characteristic muted 1950s palette. His rugged, textured stoneware was highly acclaimed and he also designed glassware for Holmegaard and Kosta Boda, Swedish glass producers.

Lindberg succeeded Kåge as Creative Director of Gustavsberg, a post he held between 1949 and 1957, and later between 1972 and 1980. He was a senior lecturer at the University College of Arts, Crafts and Design between 1957 and 1970, and won many awards at the Milan Triennales.

PUNGO (POUCH) VASE (1953)
MANUFACTURER: Gustavsberg
SPECIFICATION: Bone china vase, 25cm in height.

The elegance and purity of the 'Pungo' vase are in stark contrast to Lindberg's more whimsical and folksy designs in earthware. Like many of his designs of this period, the vase is asymmetric in form and clearly inspired by natural, organic shapes.

Stig Lindberg

POTTERY TEXTILE (1947)

MANUFACTURER: Originally produced for Nordiska Kompaniet; now reissued by Design House Stockholm in association with Ljundbergs Textiltryck

SPECIFICATION: Printed cotton. Currently available made up into cushions, bags, runners and placemats.

'Pottery' was one of two textiles Lindberg designed in 1947 for an exhibition curated by Astrid Sampe, the head of textiles at the NK (Nordiska Kompaniet) department store in Stockholm. The other was 'Lustgarden' (Garden of Eden). Much of Lindberg's work had a strong pictorial element, showing influences from folk art and the work of contemporary artists such as Marc Chagall and the surrealists. In addition to ceramics, glassware and textile design, Lindberg also created illustrations for children's books.

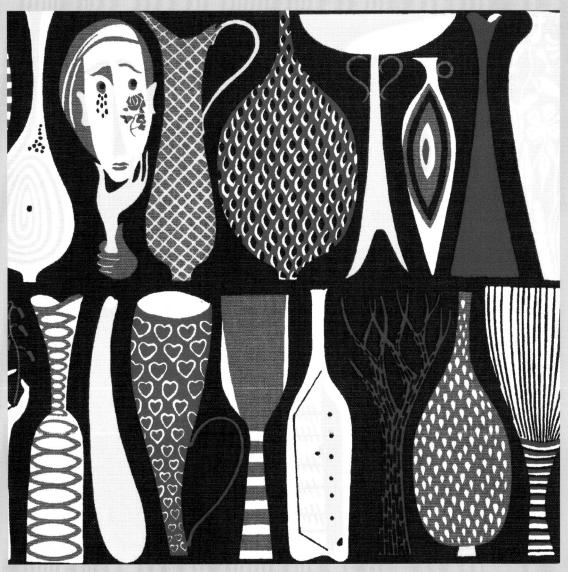

Per Lütken

DANISH GLASSWARE DESIGNER
(1916–98)

Unlike many Scandinavian modern designers, who often embraced several different disciplines, Per Lütken worked exclusively in glass. His deep appreciation of the material and the glass-making process resulted in a unique body of work, including both experimental or studio pieces and ranges of glassware for mass production. Lütken was no rarefied designer expecting others to resolve technical difficulties. By working closely with the glass-makers who translated his ideas into real products he was able to explore the full potential of his chosen medium.

After completing his studies at the School of Arts and Crafts in Copenhagen in 1937, Lütken worked as a freelance designer before succeeding Jacob Bang as creative director and chief designer at the Holmegaard glassworks, where he was to remain throughout his long career. His early work was simple uncoloured glass in a classical style. In the mid 1950s, however, after he visited the 1954 Milan Triennale, he began to produce more organic forms and introduce colour.

Much of Lütken's best-known and most collectable work dates from the 1950s and 1960s and is typical of the Scandinavian modern aesthetic. Bowls and vases were often weighty, emphasising the plasticity of molten glass. Asymmetry was another common theme. In the 1960s his glassware was often more textured and less pure, reflecting the trend for rusticity in design. He carried on working at Holmegaard for many years, experimenting with new forms and new types of colouring.

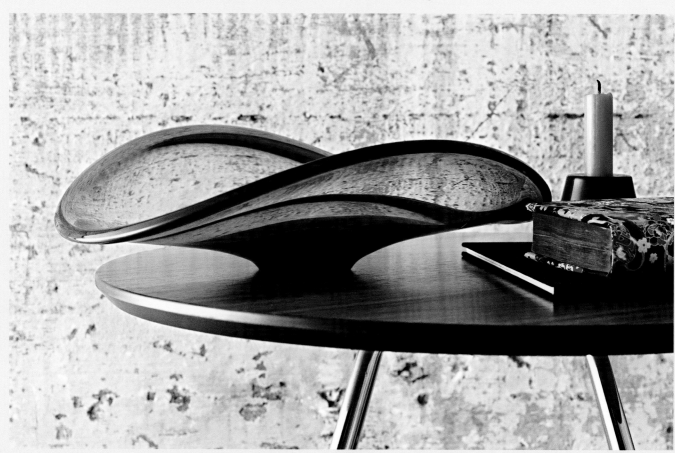

VASES AND BOWLS (1950s)
MANUFACTURER: Holmegaard
SPECIFICATION: Glass.

Lütken's belief in 'living glass' is exemplified by the curvaceous organic forms of his designs, which capture and reveal the glass-making process. Many of his pieces were self-blown, while others were produced in close collaboration with the Holmegaard glass-makers. Lütken's glassware is highly collectable today and regularly crops up in online auctions and other sources of mid-century modern design.

Bruno Mathsson

SWEDISH FURNITURE DESIGNER AND ARCHITECT (1907–88)

'Comfortable sitting is an "art" – it ought not to be. Instead the making of chairs has to be done with such an "art" that the sitting will not be any "art".' BRUNO MATHSSON

As a furniture designer and later as an architect, Bruno Mathsson was far ahead of his time, producing work that anticipated many of the directions and preoccupations of postwar design. His furniture is still in production today.

Mathsson was born in Värnamo, the son of fourth-generation cabinetmaker Karl Mathsson, who trained him in the family business and gave him a deep appreciation for wood and the craft skills involved in furniture-making. From the outset, Mathsson was interested in new ideas and techniques. The 1930 Stockholm Exhibition introduced him to functionalism, which was a lasting influence. However, Mathsson never adopted a machine-age aesthetic. Instead he believed strongly that furniture should accommodate the natural postures of the human body and carried out many experiments into what he called 'the mechanics of sitting' to determine the form of his chairs.

An early design, the 'Grasshopper' chair (1931), designed for the reception area at Värnamo hospital was so radical in appearance, with its webbed seat and arched frame, that it was reportedly hidden away from view. In 1933 he began working on the design of his most famous chair, originally known as the 'Arbetsstol' (Working Chair) and since renamed 'Eva'. Like all of Mathsson's designs, it was manufactured by his father's firm. Although it has been widely supposed that the 'Arbetsstol' was influenced by similar designs by Alvar Aalto, Mathsson's innovative use of webbing and laminated bentwood predate Aalto's endeavours by several years.

Mathsson began to attract international attention when his furniture was exhibited first in Paris in 1937 and subsequently at the Swedish

Pavilion at the World's Fair in New York in 1939. Edgar Kaufmann, Jr., who was so influential in establishing Scandinavian modern in the United States, recommended that the 'Arbetsstol' be bought for the public areas of MoMA.

During the 1940s Mathsson's furniture was a commercial success in the United States. Although Mathsson was approached by other manufacturers keen to produce and market his

Bruno Mathsson

designs, he continued to produce, market and distribute his work himself. In the 1960s he collaborated with the Danish mathematician Piet Hein in the design of the 'Super Ellipse' table.

The second important strand of Mathsson's career was architecture. Self-taught, an important influence on his buildings was a tour he made of major cities in the United States in the late 1940s. Mathsson's architectural work was as pioneering as his furniture. His plans were simple and there was a great emphasis on expanses of glass to blur the boundaries between inside and out. He also designed underfloor heating, double- and triple-glazed windows and experimented with passive solar gain half a century before environmental concerns became a preoccupation of designers.

EVA CHAIR (1933–6)
MANUFACTURER: Originally produced by Karl Mathsson; now by Bruno Mathsson International
SPECIFICATION: Seat frame in solid birch, with under-frame and arms in bent laminated beech. Covered in plaited linen webbing, plaited leather or fully upholstered; different colours available.

The 'Eva' chair or 'Arbetsstol' (Working Chair) is one of the pioneering designs of Scandinavian modern. Compared to Aalto's designs of the same period, which it resembles, it has a more undulating form and reflects Mathsson's experiments into the ergonomics of sitting. Mathsson went on to develop a range of chairs in the same idiom, including the 'Pernilla' chaise longue.

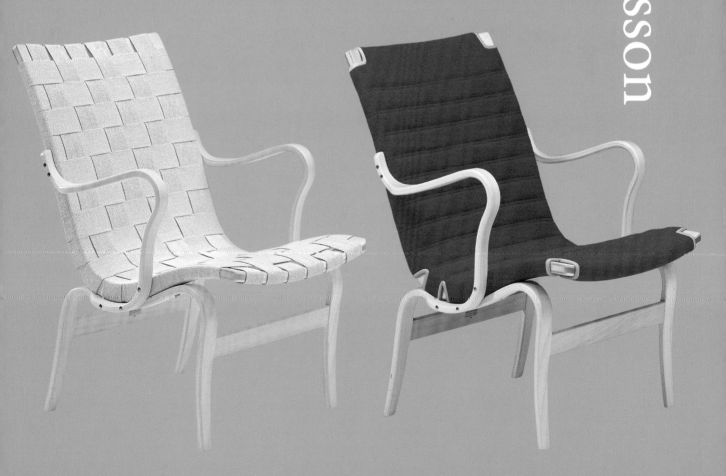

Børge Mogensen

DANISH FURNITURE DESIGNER
(1914–72)

Trained under Kaare Klint, as were many Danish furniture designers of the period, Børge Mogensen was noted for his simple, functional designs, many of which were reworkings of traditional forms, an approach strongly advocated by Klint. Klint was also famous for his research into the basic dimensions and postures of the human body and for his insistence that furniture should be designed with these parameters in mind. In his later work, Mogensen took such research further, developing modular storage systems that could be customised according to individual need.

Mogensen studied at the School of Arts and Crafts in Copenhagen from 1936 to 1938, then subsequently at the Royal Danish Academy of Fine Arts. Here he was taught by Klint, and went on to work as his assistant after graduation in 1941. In the early 1940s Mogensen was also closely associated with the Danish Cooperative Wholesale Societies, who promoted functional designs for everyday use – furniture for people who appreciated simplicity but who would have found more overtly modernist design too challenging.

Mogensen's own designs very much reflected the influence of Klint. An armchair designed in 1944 was based on the English Windsor chair and the 'J-39 Shaker' chair has obvious antecedents – Klint was a great admirer of Shaker furniture. The 'Model no. 1789' sofa, one of Mogensen's best-known designs, which dates from 1945, is an updating of the classic Knole sofa, and features a side that can be dropped down. Mogensen was a prolific furniture designer and exhibited work every year at the Cabinetmakers' Guild Exhibition in Copenhagen. During the 1950s he worked with the weaver Lis Ahlmann and produced a number of textile designs, simple checked and striped patterns that complemented the uncluttered lines of his furniture.

More radical, perhaps, was the research Mogensen carried out into the contemporary home and lifestyle, particularly the problem of storage. In 1953, he designed a room set, 'This is Where We Live', which included a workbench and sewing table, prefiguring the multi-purpose livings spaces of today. He advocated building in shelving and storage as part of the room, and conducted a series of studies, measuring everyday possessions, from cutlery to shirts, and estimating what the average family owned, in order to come up with standardised measurements for the width and depth of drawers and shelves. This research, which was published as a manual, formed the basis of two storage systems Mogensen designed in collaboration with Grethe Meyer, the 'Boligens Byggeskabe' (Construction Cupboards of the House) in 1956 and the well-known system 'Oresund', which first appeared in 1957 and was developed for a further ten years.

J-39 SHAKER CHAIR (1944)
MANUFACTURER: FDB
SPECIFICATION: Beech frame, papercord seat.

A Danish updating of a classic Shaker design, this chair reflects Mogensen's absorption of Klint's teachings. Like all of Mogensen's furniture, it displays a high degree of craftsmanship.

MODEL NO 1789 SOFA (1945)
MANUFACTURER: Fritz Hansen
SPECIFICATION: Matt or lacquered beech frame; cushions upholstered in fabric or leather, with or without buttons; one side of the sofa drops down, held in position by leather ties.

The spoke back sofa represents a simplified version of two traditional antecedents – the turned spindles of the frame recall the Windsor chair and the drop-down side is reminiscent of the Knole sofa. Designed at a time when much upholstered furniture was heavy and bulky, the clean lines and slender form of this sofa represented a significant break with the past.

Antti Nurmesniemi

FINNISH DESIGNER
(1927–2003)

Antti Nurmesniemi's design work, which included furniture, lamps and household objects, as well as telephones and trains, was created within the context of the Finnish modern architectural movement that grew up after the war. From 1947 to 1950 he studied at the University of Art and Design in Helsinki and then travelled to Stockholm and Copenhagen, seeing at firsthand the new organic forms of modern Swedish and Danish design. In the early 1950s he worked for an architectural practice that promoted a rational approach, designing furniture and interiors.

In 1953 Nurmesniemi married Vuokko Eskolin, a fashion and textile designer who became artistic director of Marimekko the same year and was to become famous for her handling of strong colour, bold geometric patterning and youthful designs. Three years later he set up his own design practice in Helsinki. One of his first successes was a simple steel coffee pot, available in three colours, red, yellow and light blue (all of which were chosen by Vuokko).

Nurmesniemi designed for a number of leading Scandinavian companies, including Artek and Arabia in Finland. Early furniture, notably the Sauna stool, designed in 1952, was in wood, but his most famous designs, which dated from the 1960s, featured a minimal use of steel. One, the prize-winning 'Triennale' chair (1960), has recently been re-issued.

BELOW Nurmesniemi's brightly coloured enamelled coffee pots were an early success.

Antti Nurmesniemi

MODEL NO. 001 CHAISE LONGUE (1968)
MANUFACTURER: Designed for Vuokko, the
company founded by Nurmesniemi's wife in 1964
SPECIFICATION: Chaise longue resting on
chromed steel supports upholstered in fabric
designed by Vuokko Nurmesniemi.

Nurmesniemi's chaise longue is an elegant
rationalist abstraction of a traditional form – a
reclining chair reduced to its bare essentials. The
design was produced for the company founded
by his wife in 1964 and provided a means of
displaying one of her distinctive textile designs.

Sven Palmqvist

**SWEDISH GLASS DESIGNER
(1906–84)**

'With glass you are able to sculpt with light and with help from the sun you can paint with colours.' SVEN PALMQVIST

Sven Palmqvist was born in the glass-making district of southern Sweden and began his training in 1928 at the engraving school at Orrefors glassworks. This was followed by studies in Stockholm at the University College of Arts, Crafts and Design and other institutions, as well as periods spent abroad acquiring knowledge and expertise at glass-making centres in Paris, Italy, Czechoslovakia and the United States.

In 1936 Palmqvist returned to Orrefors where he remained until 1972. His great contribution to Scandinavian glassware was not simply the graceful functional forms he produced, but also the innovative techniques that he devised and which vastly extended the creative potential of the medium.

The first of these was 'Kraka'. The technique involved sandwiching a fishnet-patterned layer of glass between two layers of clear glass, giving a subtle textural effect and a soft modulation of tone or colour. Examples of glass produced using this technique were exhibited in Paris in 1937 and at the World's Fair in New York in 1939.

Palmqvist's next technical breakthrough came in 1954 when he devised a way of spinning molten glass in a mould. The centrifugal force pressed the glass to the outer wall of the mould and removed the necessity for hand finishing. Examples of Fuga glassware exhibited at the Milan Triennale in 1957 won him a gold medal and Grand Prix.

In parallel with his development of 'Fuga', he was also experimenting with a decorative technique that created the effect of glass mosaic by isolating coloured glass within air channels. 'Ravenna' glassware, which displays this method, is some of his richest and most poetic work.

FUGA GLASSWARE (1950s)
MANUFACTURER: Orrefors
SPECIFICATION: Glass.

Palmqvist's characteristic graceful forms are enhanced by strong colour. He invented the technique that gives the range its name. It involves spinning molten glass in a mould so that the glass is pressed to the outer walls by centrifugal force, obviating the need for hand-finishing.

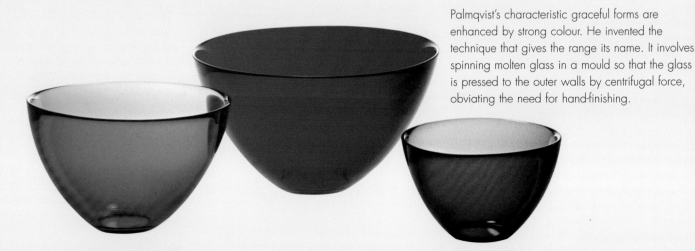

KRAKA GLASSWARE (1940s)
MANUFACTURER: Orrefors
SPECIFICATION: Glass.

The beautifully modulated and textural effect of this glassware
is achieved by sandwiching a layer of fishnet-patterned glass,
coloured or plain, between two layers of plain glass.

Verner Panton

DANISH ARCHITECT AND DESIGNER
(1926–98)

'The main purpose of my work is to provoke people into using their imagination. Most people spend their lives living in dreary, grey-beige conformity, mortally afraid of using colours. By experimenting with lighting, colours, textiles and furniture and utilizing the latest technologies, I try to show new ways, to encourage people to use their imagination and make their surroundings more exciting.' VERNER PANTON

Within the Scandinavian modern idiom, particularly its Danish variant, Verner Panton is something of an anomaly. Throughout his career, he displayed a very un-Danish approach in his rejection of traditional forms and the use of natural materials, pursuing instead a space-age aesthetic in brash new synthetics. Nevertheless, his concern for unity in design and fondness for organic curves owes a great deal to his Scandinavian origins. Something of an enfant terrible, he was described by fellow Danish designer Poul Henningsen as 'stubborn and forever young'.

Panton, the son of an innkeeper, trained at the Odense Polytechnic and subsequently studied architecture at the Royal Danish Academy of Fine Arts, where he graduated in 1951. The following two years were spent working in Arne Jacobsen's office, where he assisted in the experiments that led to the production of the 'Ant' chair. After a protracted tour of Europe, he returned to Copenhagen and set up his own practice.

From the outset, Panton pushed at the boundaries of convention, his playful imagination often a step ahead of what could be technically achieved. One of his first commissions was to rebuild and redesign an inn in a small town on the island of Funen where he had grown up. His bold all-red interior created a sensation, as did his 'Cone' chair, which was used for seating.

Other innovative interiors followed, including a number of exhibition designs. His redesign of the Astoria Restaurant in Trondheim in 1960 displayed what was becoming a characteristic palette of bright colours, along with unusual fantastic forms influenced by Op-Art. A decade later, Panton's psychedelic interior for the 'Visiona II' exhibition was a huge draw at the Cologne Furniture Fair. This fantasy landscape blurred the distinction between architecture, interior and furniture, with three-dimensional carpeting, grotto-like enclosures and rippling forms in brilliant colour adding up to a total sensory experience.

Throughout his career, Panton designed furniture, lamps and textiles for companies such as Fritz Hansen and Louis Poulsen. One of his most iconic chairs, the 'Panton' or 'Stacking' chair, arose out of an early design, the 'S-chair' (1955), which was made of a single piece of cantilevered plywood. The 'Panton' chair was similar in form but the basic concept was to make it in plastic. It took years of development before it was finally put into production, by which time Panton had settled in Switzerland.

Later designs explored pure geometric forms. If anything, Panton's work is more successful and popular today than ever before, as the true originality of his forward-looking and optimistic approach is appreciated by a new generation.

CONE CHAIR (1958)

MANUFACTURER: Originally Plus-Linje; now produced by Vitra

SPECIFICATION: Conical body made of laminate, mounted on a satin stainless steel base; polyurethane upholstery. The chair pivots on its base.

One of Panton's early radical designs, the 'Cone' chair caused an international sensation. The form recalls an ice-cream cornet and the reference is typical of Panton's Pop-inspired aesthetic. The chair was originally designed for the theatrical all-red interior of the Komigen inn, Panton's first major commission and was later put into production by Plus-Linje.

PANTHELLA (1970)

MANUFACTURER: Louis Poulsen

SPECIFICATION: Hemispherical shade made of high-pressure moulded opal acrylic; base and housing in polycarbonate; steel stem; available in floor and table versions, the table version with a slightly smaller shade.

ORIGINAL COLOURS: Originally produced in a number of colours; now produced solely in white.

The refined form of the 'Panthella' lamp is one of Panton's more restrained lighting designs. The hemispherical mushroom-like shade is supported by a delicate stem that flares out at the base. Both shade and base act as reflectors, creating a soft quality of ambient light.

Verner Panton

PANTON CHAIR (1960)

MANUFACTURER: Vitra for Herman Miller; reissued 1990

SPECIFICATION: Back, seat and base in single continuous plastic form. Available in three versions. The 'Classic' version has a hard foam plastic shell and a lacquered finish; the 'Standard' version comes in satin-finished through-coloured polypropylene and the 'Junior' version is 25% smaller. 'Classic' and 'Standard' versions in red, white and black; 'Junior' comes in seven colours.

The 'Panton' chair has come into its own in the last couple of decades with advances in plastics technology. The first cantilevered design to be made out of plastic, difficulties associated with its production meant that although the design concept dates back to 1960, the first chairs were not made until 1967. The following year, the design won great acclaim at the Cologne Furniture Fair. Subsequent developments in plastics allowed the chair to be produced in greater numbers but it was eventually withdrawn in 1979 because the plastics then available were not sufficiently strong. In 1990 Vitra reissued the chair in both polypropylene and polyurethane hard foam.

Shaped to fit the human form like a glove, the sexy curves and glossy finish recall automotive design. A new version, scaled to suit children, has recently been issued.

Sigurd Persson

SWEDISH DESIGNER
(1914–2003)

Like many Scandinavian modern designers, Sigurd Persson, who is chiefly known for his metal ware and jewellery, was born into a craft tradition. Between the ages of 14 and 23 he learned silversmithing from his father, before going on to study at Munich, and later at the University College of Arts, Crafts and Design in Stockholm.

After Persson finished his training in 1942 he set up his own workshop in Stockholm. Early work was focused on cutlery and jewellery, often in silver. In 1949 he also set up an industrial design practice, and the two strands – the creation of one-off art pieces and the design of utility products for commercial production – ran in parallel throughout his long and successful career. Simplicity and a sculptural quality were hallmarks of his work in either sphere.

In the 1950s, Persson designed stainless steel dishes for Silver & Stål, which reflected contemporary work in ceramics, both in their functionalism and beauty. Other projects included cutlery for SAS, glassware for the Swedish glassworks Kosta, as well as rings, bracelets, necklaces and other pieces of jewellery and silverware, many of which are exhibited in international museums and collections. In 1987 the Royal Society of Arts in London made him Honorary Designer for Industry and in 1993 he was named a Fellow of the RSA. His silversmithing work in particular was highly influential and helped reestablish the craft in the United States.

VEGETABLE DISHES (1953)
MANUFACTURER: Silver & Stål
SPECIFICATION: Stainless steel.

These stainless steel dishes echo work being done in ceramics in the 1950s. The dishes are designed to stack and double up to form lids. At the same time, the organic form and sculptural quality add something extra to the basic functionalism. Persson's background and training as a silversmith informed his designs for commercial production.

DANISH DESIGNER
(1919–2008)

Jens Quistgaard

'The craftsman who designs for mass production must first of all know and appreciate his material.' JENS QUISTGAARD

Quistgaard was born in Copenhagen, his father a well-known sculptor who taught at the Royal Danish Academy of Fine Arts, and his mother a painter. Early on Quistgaard developed a particular fascination with wood, which never left him, but he also learned to work in clay, iron and steel, amongst other materials. As a child he made his own toys from scraps of wood his father brought home; at the age of 14 his Christmas present, which he himself had requested, was a forge and anvil. While Quistgaard received little formal training, being largely self-taught or instructed by his father, he also served an apprenticeship at Georg Jensen's silversmith studio.

After the Second World War, during which he served in the Danish resistance, Quistgaard worked independently as a designer, producing work characterised by fluid, organic forms and a mastery of materials. Many of these designs were inspired by traditional antecedents. In 1954 he was awarded the prestigious Lunning Prize.

The same year his work came to the attention of Ted Nierenberg, an American entrepreneur and engineer. During a visit to Copenhagen, Nierenberg saw flatware designed by Quistgaard in a museum and was struck by its unusual combination of materials – hand-forged stainless steel with teak handles. He persuaded Quistgaard that it would be possible to put his designs into mass production and the seminal company Dansk was founded.

Dansk, which became famous for bringing Scandinavian modern homewares to the American market, was originally based in New York State. For over thirty years Quistgaard was responsible for designing most of the company's output, working from his studio in Copenhagen.

As a designer of everyday products, Quistgaard is notable for his instinctive appreciation of the inherent qualities of different materials, often used in combination, and his expressive, organic forms. Many of his best-known and most sought-after designs, including ice buckets, salad bowls and peppermills are made of wood, particularly teak, but he also designed cookware, candle holders and cutlery in a range of other materials, including enamelled steel and cast-iron. Blending traditional craftsmanship and forms with a fluid, sculptural approach, Quistgaard's mass-produced domestic products retain an enduring human quality.

Quistgaard carried on working well into his eighties. In addition to products for the home – some 4,500 in total throughout his career – he was also involved in graphic and architectural design.

LEFT Quistgaard excelled at the design of everyday objects. His iconic teak ice bucket can be seen at the extreme right of the picture, while the coloured enamelled cookware are also his designs.

Jens Quistgaard

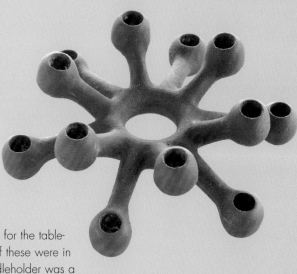

SPIDER CANDLEHOLDER (MID 1950s)
MANUFACTURER: Dansk
SPECIFICATION: Cast-iron with black patination.

Quistgaard designed an enormous range of objects for the table-top, including many different candleholders. Most of these were in cast-iron, with a rough black finish. The Spider candleholder was a popular design from the mid-1950s. The candleholder was designed to hold 12 thin tapers – many of Quistgaard's candleholders similarly feature multiple points of light.

CONGO ICE BUCKET (1960)
MANUFACTURER: Dansk
SPECIFICATION: Teak.

One of Quistgaard's best-known designs, the form of this teak ice bucket was inspired by the hulls of Viking ships. Quistgaard had a particular fondness for wood and designed many items in teak, including salad bowls, cutting boards, serving dishes and trays. Many of his bowls were made from radial staves of wood, an economical use of the material.

KOBENSTYLE COOKWARE (1954)
MANUFACTURER: Dansk
SPECIFICATION: Range of cooking pans, including lidded casseroles and skillets, made of steel enamelled in a range of vibrant colours, including bright red, turquoise and yellow.

The 'Kobenstyle' range of oven-to-table cookware, released by Dansk in 1956, epitomises Quistgaard's approach. The idea was to create a range of pots that would be lighter than cast-iron and so affordable, as well as attractive enough to be placed on the table. Previously, enamelled steel had a reputation for shoddiness. This range, sturdy and beautifully designed, gave it a new popularity. The fine organic curves of the handles display Quistgaard's sensitivity to material quality. The lids are designed so that they can be upturned and used as trivets.

Eero Saarinen

FINNISH-AMERICAN ARCHITECT AND DESIGNER (1910–61)

While not strictly speaking a Scandinavian modern designer, Eero Saarinen represents an important bridge between that aesthetic and mid-century design in America, a connection forged chiefly at the Cranbrook Academy of Art in Michigan, co-founded by his father, Eliel Saarinen.

Eliel Saarinen, architect, town planner and one of the most important figures in Finnish design, had emigrated with his family to the United States in 1922. A decade later he launched the Cranbrook Academy, which was to become America's leading design school. Saarinen's wife was a textile designer and sculptor, his daughter was a designer and interior designer and his son, Eero would become an important architect and designer in his own right. The entire family contributed to the design of the Cranbook campus, which was conceived as a total environment, from the landscaped setting down to the design of decorative objects.

Saarinen's legacy was not only one of the most talented generation of American designers of the twentieth century, which numbered among its ranks Charles and Ray Eames, Florence Knoll and Harry Bertoia, but a tempering of European modernism with the humanistic ideals embedded in the Scandinavian approach to design. Arguably it was this dissemination of the Scandinavian ethos that helped ensure favourable critical reception and the eventual popular success of Scandinavian modern design in postwar America.

Eero Saarinen studied sculpture in Paris and then went on to study architecture at Yale, finishing his studies in 1934. After extensive travels, he returned to Cranbrook, where he taught for a while and collaborated with his father on a number of architectural projects. Charles Eames was a close friend, as was Florence Knoll. In 1940 Saarinen and Eames won first prize at the Museum of Modern Art's 'Organic Design in Home Furnishings' competition for a moulded plywood chair they co-designed. While Eames subsequently went on to work for Herman Miller, Saarinen's furniture designs were produced for Knoll Associates. He established his own architectural practice in 1950.

In a career cut short by his untimely death at the age of 51, Saarinen exerted a huge influence on the direction of postwar American design and architecture. His most famous building is the TWA terminal at Kennedy International Airport, New York, a work that echoes the sculptural organic forms of his furniture. Other major projects displayed different stylistic approaches, an apparent inconsistency for which he was criticised in some quarters.

Saarinen retained close contact with Finland throughout his life. He served on the jury for the Sydney Opera House competition and was instrumental in the selection of Jørn Utzon.

RIGHT 'Tulip' table and chairs, designed by Eero Saarinen, 1955–7.

Eero Saarinen

WOMB CHAIR (1946–8)
MANUFACTURER: Knoll
SPECIFICATION: Chair constructed of foam over a moulded, reinforced fibreglass shell; base of bent steel rods with polished chrome finish or matt black powder-coated finish; two separate cushions for seat and back. Three sizes: standard, medium and small, with standard and medium having accompanying ottoman. Available upholstered in a wide range of Knoll fabrics and leathers.

Designed in response to Florence Knoll's request for a chair she could 'curl up in', the 'Womb' chair offers just that sense of physical and psychological security. Unlike traditional easy or armchairs, the design is clean and uncluttered without sacrificing any degree of comfort. The 'Womb' chair reflects the organic humanistic sensibility that Saarinen was schooled in and has become a classic of mid-century design, remaining in continuous production.

TULIP CHAIR (1955–7)
MANUFACTURER: Knoll
SPECIFICATION: Moulded fibreglass seat shell with a reinforced plastic bonded finish; cast aluminium base with coated finish; loose foam upholstered seat cushion; also available with a fully upholstered inner shell. Base and shell available in black, white and platinum. Upholstered in a range of Knoll fabrics and leathers.

The 'Tulip' chair was conceived as part of a range of 'Pedestal' furniture, which includes tables and side tables. The swivelling chair is an essay in visual unity: Saarinen's aim was to clear up what he called the 'slum of legs' that was a feature of so much modern furniture design. Constructed in two parts and available with or without arms, the base is plastic-coated to give the appearance that the chair is a single form.

The chair is now an icon of post-war design and has won many awards. Combined with the matching table, the chairs have great sculptural presence.

Astrid Sampe

SWEDISH TEXTILE DESIGNER
(1909–2002)

Like many Scandinavian modern designers, Astrid Sampe came from a long craft tradition and was born into a family of textile weavers that went back several generations. Between 1928 and 1932 she trained at the University College of Arts, Crafts and Design in Stockholm, which included an exchange at the Royal College of Art in London.

After completing her studies, Sampe was hired by Nordiska Kompaniet (The Nordic Company), a large department store based in Stockholm and Gothenberg. NK, as the store is generally known, appointed her head of their newly created textile studio in 1937, where she was to remain until the studio was dissolved in 1971. Here, in addition to creating her own designs, she pioneered the concept of 'signed textiles', a collection of prints by named designers, aimed at the contract market. Stig Lindberg was among those who designed for NK, on Sampe's instigation, as was Sven Markelius.

In 1939 Sampe collaborated with Sven Markelius on the design of the Swedish Pavilion at the New York World's Fair, where her textiles attracted much attention. Later, in 1947, when the American furniture company Knoll was setting up its own textile department, Sampe was one of the six designers recruited to their 'International Group'. Markelius and Lindberg were two of the other members. Previously, Knoll had been unable to source the right sort of upholstery fabrics for their ranges of contemporary furniture and had been using suiting acquired from British tailors.

Sampe exhibited widely throughout her career and was the recipient of many awards. In 1949, following her contribution to the 'Modern Swedish Home' exhibition at the London Building Centre, she was made Honorary Royal Designer for Industry by the Royal Society of Arts in London. She won a Grand Prix at the Milan Triennale in 1954. In 1961 she was commissioned by the United Nations to design carpets for the Dag Hammarsjöld Library.

Sampe's work, whether for domestic linens, carpets or contract textiles, represented an updating of craft tradition for commercial production. Her designs display a confident handling of colour and strong geometric or abstract patterning. At the same time she was a keen innovator, and in the 1960s was the first Swedish designer to weave in fibreglass. In the late 1970s, after she had established her own studio, she began experimenting with computer-based patterns.

Astrid Sampe

LAZY LINES TEXTILE (1950s)
MANUFACTURER: Originally produced by
Knoll International; reproduced in 1985 by
Ljungbergs Textiltryck
SPECIFICATION: Screen-printed plain-weave
cotton.

This design is one of a series of patterns Sampe
created for Knoll as part of their 'International
Group' of textile designers. When Knoll began
manufacturing and marketing contemporary
furniture, patterned upholstery fabrics were
typically floral or brocade and the company was
initially forced to import sober suitings from British
tailors in order not to compromise the clean lines
of the designs they produced. Simple striped
patterns, a feature of traditional Swedish woven
textiles, gained a new lease of life with
Scandinavian modern.

Timo Sarpaneva

FINNISH DESIGNER
(1926–2006)

'Glass released me from the conventional and the three-dimensional. It opened its deepest reaches to me and took me on a journey to the fourth dimension. I understood the opportunities that clear, transparent glass gives to an artist and designer.' TIMO SARPANEVA

A master of many materials, but pre-eminent in glass, Timo Sarpaneva was among those who helped to establish Finland's reputation for contemporary design in the postwar period. The grandson of a blacksmith, Sarpaneva studied at the University of Art and Design in Helsinki, graduating in 1948. Two years later he went to work for the Iittala glassworks as product designer and head of exhibitions and it was here that he created his most innovative designs.

During a long association with Iittala, Sarpaneva experimented with different methods, producing designs for everyday use as well as art glass. The 'i-Glass' range of utility glassware, which won a Grand Prix at the 1957 Milan Triennale, came in evocative watery colours that elevated everyday products into objects of beauty. Sarpaneva also designed the packaging and the logo for the range, which was unusual at the time. Soon after the logo was adopted by Iittala as the company trademark.

In the 1960s Sarpaneva worked increasingly in frosted glass, creating sculptural pieces that evoked the Nordic landscape. One particular series of vases, 'Finlandia', was produced in moulds roughly carved from alder wood. The resulting pieces were patterned by the wood and the wooden moulds in turn were burnt by the molten glass, which meant that the next time they were used a different surface texture was created and no two vases were alike. The same technique was used to make the popular 'Festivo' candleholders.

Later Sarpaneva returned to the pure shapes that had been the hallmark of his work in the 1950s. The 'Arkipelago' collection, with its trapped bubbles of various sizes, evokes blocks of ice, while the 'Claritas' range, with trapped bubbles of a larger size, recalls the form of many of his sculptural pieces from the beginning of his career. In the 1990s he collaborated with Venini glassworks of Murano, where maestro Pino Signoretto realised Sarpaneva's 'Millennium Meum' glass sculptures.

Despite the fact that Sarpaneva is best known for his work in glass, he also excelled in other fields. It was textile design that won him his first international acclaim at the 1951 Milan Triennale; later he also worked in cast-iron, porcelain and graphics. His work was exhibited widely and he was the recipient of many awards. In 1963 he was made Honorary Royal Industrial Designer for Industry by the Royal Society of Arts in London and was awarded an honorary doctorate by the Royal College of Art in 1967.

I-GLASS RANGE (1956)
MANUFACTURER: Iittala
SPECIFICATION: Range of glassware;
17 pieces including decanters and tumblers.

'Because glass is the material of space, it is best
suited as a material to be given to light.'
TIMO SARPANEVA

The 'i-Glass' range was a popular and critical
success. The pure forms, accentuated by
wonderfully evocative shades of blue, grey, green
and purple, brought art within the reach of
ordinary households. The small lip on the
decanters, along with their curved organic shape,
give them the appearance of stylised birds.

Timo Sarpaneva

CAST-IRON POT (1960)
MANUFACTURER: Originally W. Rosenlew & Co;
now produced by Iittala
SPECIFICATION: Enamelled cast-iron; detachable teak handle.

Sarpaneva's grandfather was a blacksmith and he had grown up
fascinated by the forge. This cooking pot, a reworking of a
traditional design, features a detachable handle that you can use
either to lift the pot or open the lid. The pot featured on a Finnish
postage stamp, one of a series celebrating the best of Finnish design.

Jørn Utzon

DANISH ARCHITECT AND DESIGNER
(1918–2008)

Jørn Utzon is world-famous as the designer of the iconic Sydney Opera House. Utzon won the opera house competition in 1957 but there were controversies right from the start. Eero Saarinen, who was on the jury, declared the proposals a work of genius, even though Utzon's submissions did not meet the competition rules. Difficulties associated with the project – particularly the technical problem of how to construct the sailing roof shells – political manoeuvrings and cost over-run saw Utzon removed from the scheme before its completion. He never returned to Australia and was not invited to the building's opening ceremony.

Utzon had trained as an architect at the Royal Danish Academy of Fine Arts, graduating in 1942. Subsequently he worked for Gunnar Asplund before establishing his own architectural practice in 1947.

During the course of his career Utzon designed not only buildings but also furniture, glassware and lights. His 'Floating Dock' furniture for Fritz Hansen, a modular range of tables and chairs, was based on an interlocking system of triangular-section aluminium components.

Utzon has been the recipient of numerous awards, including a Gold Medal from the Royal Institute of British Architects in 1978. In 2003 he was awarded the world's most prestigious architectural prize, the Pritzker.

OPERA HOUSE PENDANT LAMP (1960s)
MANUFACTURER: Light Years (since 2006)
SPECIFICATION: Pendant lamp composed of seven overlapping metal shades; white lacquered finish.

Echoing the segmented form of Sydney's most famous landmark, the 'Opera House' pendant is a variation on the multi-shade principle of light diffusion. The pendant comprises seven asymmetrical shades formed into soft organic curves, secured at the base by four mounting screws. Light is directed both downwards and through the gaps between the overlapping layers, adding to the decorative effect.

Poul Volther

DANISH ARCHITECT AND FURNITURE DESIGNER (1923–2001)

A leading architect in Denmark, Poul Volther is best known internationally for one particular design, the 'Corona' chair, one of the icons of Scandinavian modern design. While this design is a clear departure from the reworking of traditional forms that characterised the work of Danish designers such as Finn Juhl and Hans Wegner, Volther was nevertheless strongly opposed to superficial trends and fads in design and had a firm commitment to quality.

Poul Volther worked as a joiner before studying cabinet-making and architecture at the School of Arts and Crafts in Copenhagen. After graduation he set up his own design and architectural practice in 1949. He was also an influential teacher at a number of Copenhagen design institutes.

While the 'Corona' chair, which Volther designed in 1961, breaks with the Danish modern tradition of working in wood, an earlier prototype of the design did feature a solid oak frame. When the chair was eventually launched, to great acclaim, in 1964, the frame was made of chromed steel. The original version was upholstered in tomato red leather – Erik Jørgensen, the company which has produced the chair since the 1960s was originally a saddlemakers.

A key feature of the design are the floating elements that comprise the seat and back, gently curved shells that provide precisely the right support for the body and which can also be used as armrests. These were said to be inspired by the elliptical phases of a solar eclipse, hence the name. At the same time there are obvious organic references to the spine and ribs.

The streamlined, almost dematerialised form of the chair has made it a popular choice for film sets and videos. The chair was also among the furnishings chosen for the EU summit of European heads of state, held in Copenhagen in December 2002.

CORONA CHAIR (1961)
MANUFACTURER: Erik Jørgensen
SPECIFICATION: Seat and back made from four moulded plywood shells covered with moulded polyurethane foam; legs and support in matt chromed steel. Upholstered in a choice of fabric or leather; accompanying footstool.

Hans Wegner

DANISH DESIGNER
(1914–2007)

'Many foreigners have asked me how we made the Danish style. And I've answered that it... was rather a continuous process of purification, and for me of simplification, to cut down to the simplest possible elements of four legs, a seat and combined top rail and arm rest.' HANS WEGNER

Few have contributed more to the international success of Scandinavian modern than Hans Wegner. A prolific designer, responsible for over 500 chairs, he embodied the commitment to craftsmanship, simplicity and beauty that was a hallmark of mid-century Danish design. Moreover, he loved wood and his instinctive handling of the material imbues his designs with timeless vitality.

Wegner was the son of a cobbler. After an apprenticeship with a carpenter, he trained at the Technical Institute in Copenhagen before moving on to the School of Arts and Crafts. In 1940, two years after graduation, he went to work in the architectural office of Arne Jacobsen and Erik Møller as a furniture designer. Here he had the opportunity to create furniture for Aarhus City Hall, one of Denmark's most important modern buildings.

Wegner was the product of an educational system that emphasised social responsibility. He was also exposed to the new ideas of functionalism, which did away with stylistic flourishes to reveal honesty of construction and purity of form. Where he departed from other modernists was his refusal to abandon wood or the craft heritage in which he had been instructed.

In 1943 Wegner established his first office in Gentofte and began working on a series that came to be known as the 'Chinese' chairs, elegant simplifications of traditional designs that were produced by Fritz Hansen. During this period he also collaborated with Børge Mogensen, co-designing furniture for an apartment shown at the 1946 Cabinetmakers' Guild Exhibition in Copenhagen. Wegner first showed a chair at this annual exhibition in 1941 and would do so every year until 1966.

By 1949, the year in which the famous 'Round' chair was designed, Wegner had established a design practice in Copenhagen. Critical to his success as a designer was the working relationship he maintained with Johannes Hansen, a small manufacturer employing skilled craftsmen. Close collaboration between designer and manufacturer was typical of Danish furniture production; what was unusual about Wegner was that he worked alongside artisans rather than expect technical problems to be solved for him. Throughout his career Wegner worked with numerous Danish manufacturers, nearly all small-scale producers.

Of the many designs Wegner created, the most famous and successful include the 'Chinese' chair (1943), 'Peacock' chair (1947), 'Y' chair (1949), and, most notably, the 'Round' chair (1949), all carved from solid wood. The 'Teddy Bear' chair (1950) was upholstered, while the 'Ox' chair (1960) was a rare departure from wood and features bent metal legs. While Wegner pursued an ideal of perfection in his chair designs, he was often playful, too. The 'Valet' chair (1953) is a witty multi-purpose design that features a backrest in the shape of a coathanger, rails and storage under the seat – a chair that doubles up as a place to hang a suit.

The fact that Wegner's chairs are so comfortable arises out of the fact that he believed that a chair should not impose a single posture, but should allow for movement and changing position. This is particularly noticeable in the design of his easy chairs or armchairs, which remain comfortable if you curl up in them, sit upright, lean back or swing your legs over the arms. While many of his designs use a minimum amount of material, strength is never sacrificed.

Wegner was the first winner of the prestigious Lunning Prize in 1951 and the same year won a Grand Prix at the Milan Triennale. In 1959 the Royal Society of Arts in London made him Honourary Designer for Industry and he was awarded an honorary doctorate by the Royal College of Art in 1997. He continued to work into his eighties.

Hans Wegner

PP550 PEACOCK CHAIR (1947)

MANUFACTURER: Originally Johannes Hansen; since 1992 produced by PP Møbler
SPECIFICATION: Beechwood frame; seat in paper cord.

It was Finn Juhl who supposedly gave this chair its name, in reference to the fanning shape of the back with the spokes flattened above the armrests. In characteristic ergonomic fashion, those flattened portions of the spokes are not merely decorative but occur where the shoulder-blades rest against back. The chair is Wegner's reinterpretation of the classic Windsor chair.

PP19 TEDDY BEAR CHAIR (1950)

MANUFACTURER: Originally AP Stolen; now produced by PP Møbler
SPECIFICATION: Upholstered wooden frame; wood-covered handrests; exposed wooden legs; accompanying footstool.

'We must take care that everything doesn't get so dreadfully serious. We must play – but we must play seriously.' HANS WEGNER

One of the most successful and best-loved of all Wegner's chairs, the design gets its name from a remark by a critic that the arms resembled great bear paws reaching round to hug you. A reworking of the traditional wing chair form, the 'Teddy Bear' chair is supremely comfortable, supporting the body in different positions. The wooden 'paws' that animate the design with such personality serve a functional purpose – if the arms were fully upholstered, those portions would become quickly worn and soiled.

Hans Wegner

Y OR WISHBONE CHAIR (1949)
MANUFACTURER: Carl Hansen & Son
SPECIFICATION: Chair frame originally in teak, now produced in a range of woods, including maple, ash, beech, oak, cherry, walnut; seat in paper cord.

Small, light and elegant, the 'Y' chair or 'Wishbone' chair shows Wegner's mastery of form. The curve of the back legs is echoed by the semicircular top rail and the splayed wishbone support.

PP501/503 ROUND CHAIR (1949)

MANUFACTURER: Originally Johannes Hansen; produced since 1993 by PP Møbler

SPECIFICATION: Originally teak, with cane or paper cord seat; back rest with or without cane wrapping. Now produced in a range of woods including oak, ash, mahogany and cherry.

'The good chair is a task one is never completely done with.' HANS WEGNER

Wegner modestly called this design, 'the round one'. The chair was acclaimed almost as soon as it was produced. In 1950 it appeared on the cover of the American magazine *Interiors*, who described it as 'the world's most beautiful chair'. Ten years later it was chosen as seating for the televised debates between Presidential candidates John F. Kennedy and Richard Nixon. By this time it had achieved such iconic status that it was simply known as 'The Chair'.

Wegner may have been tireless in his pursuit of the perfect chair form, but he came close to achieving it with this design. The tapering legs extend upwards to support the continuous curve of the back and armrests, while the carved back supports the body in just the right place. The minimal use of material, exquisite craftsmanship and refined form give the design a timeless quality. It is beautiful from all angles.

Like many of Wegner's chairs, the 'Round' chair is as effective on its own as it is in multiples, as part of a dining set, for example. For this reason, his designs mix well with other pieces, an easy-going compatibility that is shared by the best Scandinavian modern design.

Hans Wegner

OX CHAIR (1960)

MANUFACTURER: Originally Johannes Hansen; produced since 1985 by Erik Jørgensen
SPECIFICATION: Upholstered plywood shell covered in ox hide; chromium plated steel legs; accompanying footstool.

For a designer so closely associated with wood, the 'Ox' chair represents something of a departure, with its steel legs and bulky presence. The chair was said to be Wegner's favourite. Although it was put into production by Johannes Hansen in 1960, it was withdrawn two years later because of lack of demand. By the mid-1980s its modernity was much more acceptable and it was re-issued by Erik Jørgensen.

Inspired by Picasso's drawings of bulls, the chair has a definite masculinity, almost a pugnacious look. Like all of Wegner's seat furniture, it is comfortable when you are sitting in different positions.

PP 589 BAR BENCH (1953)

MANUFACTURER: Originally Johannes Hansen; produced since 1991 by PP Møbler
SPECIFICATION: Soap-treated ash with slatted top.

Wegner originally designed this bench for the entrance hall of his home. Simple and unobtrusive, it marries practicality with the high degree of craftsmanship Wegner's work is noted for.

Tapio Wirkkala

FINNISH DESIGNER
(1915–85)

'All materials have their own unwritten laws…
the designer should aim at being in harmony
with his material.' TAPIO WIRKKALA

From laminated wood furniture, to exquisite
glassware, from hand-crafted jewellery to
domestic appliances and banknotes, there was
scarcely a design discipline or a material that
Tapio Wirkkala did not master. In many ways
Wirkkala was the quintessential Scandinavian
designer, straddling the worlds of art, craft and
design. He was also deeply inspired by nature
and traditional culture of the Sami people.

Perhaps not surprisingly given his great
versatility, Wirkkala trained as a sculptor at the
University of Art and Design in Helsinki,
graduating in 1936; he would later be its artistic
director. After winning a glassware competition
sponsored by Iittala (jointly with Kaj Franck) in
1947, he began working for the company as a
freelance designer, an association that continued
until his death. Wirkkala's innovative glassware
is amongst the best-known of his designs. His
frosted glass range 'Ultima Thule' (1968) was
highly influential.

An ambassador for Finnish design, Wirkkala
collected many awards throughout his career,
notably three Grand Prix at the 1951 Milan
Triennale and three more at the 1954 Milan
Triennale, as well as the Lunning Prize. His work
has been widely exhibited internationally.

TAPIO GLASSWARE RANGE (1954)
MANUFACTURER: Iittala
SPECIFICATION: Glass with air bubble
trapped in the stem.

Wirkkala was an innovative designer who, like Sarpaneva,
experimented tirelessly with the potential of different materials and
worked closely with the craftspeople who produced his designs.
The 'Tapio' range, which is still in production today, has a
characteristic air bubble trapped in the stem of each glass.

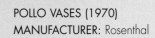

POLLO VASES (1970)
MANUFACTURER: Rosenthal
SPECIFICATION: Porcelain; in black or white and in different sizes.

Wirkkala produced a number of designs for the German manufacturer Rosenthal, including the Kurve range of flatware. One of his best loved, however, are the 'Pollo' vases, with their engaging organic form and tactility.

SCANDINAVIAN
MODERN TRADEMARKS

ABOVE Open-plan layouts make the most of light and views. Here, all-white décor makes a reflective background. Vivid cushions add accents of colour and warmth.

PREVIOUS PAGE, LEFT
Poul Kjaerholm's PK24 chaise longue,
pictured in his own home.

PREVIOUS PAGE, RIGHT
Scandinavian designers have excelled
in the production of glassware.

Open-plan Living

One of the key elements of the Scandinavian modern interior is a relatively free layout, with main living spaces merging with one another to create a seamless flow of space that makes the most of light and views. Another effect of such an arrangement is the erosion of a conventional formal hierarchy, whereby separate rooms are each assigned a different function, which was a common feature of pre-modern homes, particularly those of the well-to-do. Whereas in the past, working areas of the home were shut away behind closed doors or relegated to basements or 'backstairs' areas, and public rooms were chiefly used for entertaining guests and rarely lived in, the open plan signalled a move to a more informal, family-based style of living.

The sense of liberation that open-plan living provides in the Scandinavian modern home owes a great deal to the Funkis style, Scandinavia's interpretation of modernism. Homes were conceived as functional places, where different activities could be practically accommodated within efficiently planned and fitted spaces.

The open layout, however, was not such a radical departure in Scandinavia as it was in other parts of the world. This was because traditional Scandinavian houses, particularly in rural areas, often tended to group diverse activities within a shared common area anyway. An age-old concern for efficient use of space, coupled with a strategy of building in fixtures, fittings and storage to maximise floor area and avoid wastage was already part of the Scandinavian approach to interior design when modernism came on the scene in the late 1920s and 1930s. In a sense, the Funkis style simply

ABOVE An open staircase, minimally screened by netting, spills light down from upper levels.

its furthest extreme. Early lofts, converted from redundant warehouses and other industrial or commercial buildings, were typified by vast expanses of open space and double-height volumes, minimally partitioned, if at all, into different living zones. While many homes marketed as 'lofts' these days are much more circumscribed in terms of floor area, the free-flowing open plan layout has become ever more established, and not merely in new homes. Many houses that date back a century or more have seen partition walls removed to create a single living/eating/cooking area from what had previously been separate rooms.

Open-plan living provides flexibility, which is what we increasingly demand of our homes these days. On the other hand, the most successful open-plan layouts are those that retain spatial clues to provide a hint of separation between different activities. The clues may lie in something as simple as furniture placement, or they may take the form of more permanent fixtures, such as half-height or half-width partitions or built-in storage. Such an approach helps to strike the right balance between cosy, intimate areas and expanses of open or shared space, which all homes need to provide.

Removing unnecessary dividing walls and enlarging openings such as doorways and windows are the standard means of creating open-plan layouts. But changes to levels can be very effective, too, setting up dynamic double-height spaces and drawing light down into the interior from above. In the house Arne Jacobsen designed for himself (completed in 1950), portions of ceilings were cut away to create soaring double-height spaces whose volume was accentuated by long pendant lamps and mobiles. In Scandinavian modern, this type of spatial interpenetration is often the means of expressing an organic approach, with upright elements such as balusters extending through two floors and echoing natural forms such as tree trunks.

streamlined and updated a way of thinking about interior space that already existed. Then again, the open layout perfectly chimed with the democratic spirit inherent in Scandinavian design, which eschewed conspicuous consumption, overtly fashionable trends and grandiose effects in favour of classic, timeless designs that could be afforded by everyone. Today's flexible interiors, that allow easy shifts to be made between entertaining, relaxing, working and more private pursuits are merely the latest manifestation of an attitude to spatial planning that has firm roots in the past.

Open-plan layouts, in Scandinavia and elsewhere, became increasingly common after the Second World War. A designated dining room began to fade from view, with eating areas absorbed within living rooms or kitchens. As postwar homes were often on the small side, maintaining a separate dining room made little spatial sense. But the times had changed, too. Few households relied on the assistance of live-in servants and the social trend was for a more casual and inclusive approach to entertaining.

The arrival of loft living in the late 1970s and early 1980s saw the open plan pushed to

PRACTICALITIES

Open layouts bring certain practical considerations into play. Points to consider include the following:

♣ Removing partition walls is straightforward building work. Removing structural walls, which help to brace and support the house, requires professional assistance. Some compensating element will have to be installed to bear the load. Usually this will take the form of a rolled steel joist (RSJ) spanning the new opening. In many homes, it is not clear which walls are partitions and which are load-bearing, so it is always important to take advice from an architect or surveyor before you go ahead with the work.

♣ Open layouts can be harder to heat than individual small rooms. Underfloor heating is one of the most practical and efficient ways of heating an open-plan space, particularly one where extensive glazing reduces the available wall area further. Underfloor heating is common in Scandinavia, supplemented by the cosy focus of the wood-burning stove.

♣ Good organisation and efficient spatial planning is essential to maintain some separation between areas of activity, otherwise an open-plan interior can descend into chaos and muddle, where competing activities jostle for elbow room.

♣ It is always a good idea to balance inclusive open areas where the family can gather with more private individual retreats that offer a sense of intimacy and enclosure.

ABOVE Some spatial definition is required in open-plan layouts to signal a shift in activities. Here this is subtly provided by the change in material, with the patterned floor covering defining the kitchen area.

Indoors–Outdoors

A sense of connection to the living world is one of the great hallmarks of Scandinaivan modern. While early twentieth-century modernists took inspiration from the machine, the Nordic version of modernity that grew up between the wars never lost sight of nature. In the design of furniture, this can be seen in the use of materials such as wood, rather than metal, and in forms that were curved and organic rather than rectilinear or strictly geometric. In architecture and the design of interior spaces, natural materials and forms were also evident, as well as a desire to blur the boundaries between interior spaces and external ones. Today, as we increasingly look for more sustainable ways of living, the Scandinavian approach seems remarkably timely.

On the most basic level, the Scandinavian modern interior sponsors a connection with nature through material quality, specifically the homely warmth of wooden surfaces and finishes. Wood has always been prevalent in Nordic interiors for the simple practical reason that the region is heavily forested and timber is an abundant local resource. In the Scandinavian home, wood is widely used not only for furniture, but also flooring, panelling, architectural detailing and in the structure and external cladding of houses themselves. Another natural material often in evidence is stone, either used in a rugged unfinished state or polished and honed. Although these natural materials were often employed in a rustic or vernacular way in traditional rural buildings, in the modern Scandinavian interior, rusticity is balanced by smooth pristine surfaces, such as painted plasterwork.

The contemporary Scandinavian interior, with its open plan layout and large openings, also helps to erode the distinction between internal and external space. Over-scaled windows (highly insulated to prevent heat loss in winter) and sliding glazed doors offer external views and instant access when the weather permits. Minimal internal partitions allow the outside world to be glimpsed from different parts of the interior. At these northerly latitudes, summers are short and intense, and Scandinavians take every opportunity to enjoy outdoor living, even if the only available external space is a small terrace or balcony. Many people also maintain rural retreats deep in the countryside, often situated in areas that are inaccessible in winter. It is not unusual for these cottages and cabins to be furnished and fitted only to a basic minimum – getting away from it all entailing a return to a simpler form of existence away from modern conveniences.

Nature, too, is present in other elemental aspects of the Scandinavian home. Cosy wood-burning hearths or stoves make a cheerful focus on long winter nights, the epitome of domestic cheer, while the traditional pine-panelled sauna, where bathers sweat themselves clean in dry heat or pungent resinous steam, provides an invigorating way of getting back to basics.

BELOW Timber decking extends the house out into the surrounding landscape. Large glazed openings blur the boundaries between indoors and out.

RIGHT The ultimate integration of house and site: this modern home is literally built around a rocky outcrop, which provides a rugged contrast to the smooth plastered planes of walls and ceiling.

Light and Air

It is difficult to underestimate the importance of light in the Scandinavian interior, both natural light and those artificial sources used to supplement it. This is hardly surprising given the northerly location of these countries means that daylight is in short supply for many long months of the year. However, quantity of available light is only half of the story. Close to the Arctic Circle, winter sun comes from a low angle, glancing off the snow, while at the height of summer, days merge into long twilit nights when the sun never sets at all. The particular quality of northern light, as much as its absence or presence, is a defining characteristic of the Scandinavian interior past and present.

Long before modernism exerted its influence, Scandinavian interiors demonstrated a number of decorative and design strategies for making the most of natural light, many of which are still employed today. Pale or light-toned surfaces and finishes, together with a liberal use of white, helps to spread available light from place to place – the Scandinavian preference for light-toned wood and neutral, natural palettes for backgrounds is a case in point. So, too, is the use of mirror to reflect views and make the most of what light is available. In the contemporary home, open layouts, where dividing walls are minimised, allow light to penetrate through interior spaces, providing a dynamic and animating presence as tonal values change throughout the day.

The size, number and positioning of windows has a direct effect on the amount of natural light an interior receives. Large windows, particularly those that extend over head-height, draw in as much light as possible. Windows on upper levels also bring in a better quality of light since the views they frame consist of a greater proportion of sky, a factor that is especially critical in urban areas. Most invigorating and expansive of all is top lighting, windows or skylights set into the plane of the roof, and which spill light downwards in a dramatic fashion.

The Scandinavian thirst for light and desire to be as close to the natural world as possible adds up to homes that feature numerous, generous-sized openings. At the same time, given the harshness and length of the winter, it means that windows must be designed and constructed to a very high standard, otherwise energy will drain from the interior.

If you are opting for window walls or large picture windows, it is advisable to invest in energy-efficient low emissivity glass (low E glass) and specify high-performance windows. Unsurprisingly, given the nature of the climate, some of the most energy-efficient windows are produced in Scandinavia. The highest quality designs are wooden-framed and double- or triple-glazed. In some cases, the gaps between the glazing are filled with argon to enhance insulation; other designs feature integral blinds sandwiched between the panes, which can be operated by a handle on the outside of the frame.

Other forms of 'natural' lighting that Scandinavians never neglect are the hospitable warmth of flames flickering in a hearth or wood-burning stove, along with the magical glow of candlelight. Candlelight has a special resonance for Scandinavians and plays an important part in many winter festivities, most notably the feast of St Lucia. Candles grouped on a window sill,

LEFT The changing values of natural light animate the interior with vitality.

ABOVE Light is precious in the Scandinavian interior, where long winter months are passed in near-darkness.

RIGHT Expanses of glazing bathe the interior in natural light on all sides. The over-scaled pendant creates a soft diffusion of artificial light over the dining table.

table top or mantelpiece, or lighting a chandelier, add seasonal cheer.

Given the importance of light in the northern interior, it is small wonder that many Scandinavian designers have excelled at the design of light fittings. Many of the most famous of these, including Poul Henningsen's 'PH' series for the Danish manufacturer Louis Poulsen, or the folded paper shades produced by Le Klint, exhibit organic, natural forms and are specifically constructed to diffuse the glare of bright incandescent bulbs. Hung over dining tables, they provide an intimate focus for dining and a glowing point of interest. The same sculptural, animated quality is also displayed in task lights. A particular example is the clean-lined 'AJ' (Visor) light designed by Arne Jacobsen, which has an eager forward tilt. As in furniture design, the Scandinavian approach to the design of light fittings is to infuse them with a quality of approachability and human warmth.

A successful lighting scheme entails more than choosing well-designed fittings. The number and positioning of light sources is critical when creating an atmospheric interior and supporting everyday functions and routines safely and efficiently.

As far as generating a sympathetic mood is concerned, a key strategy is to multiply the number of light sources and conceal them wherever possible to avoid glare. Uplighting is literally uplifting. Directing light so that it reflects off the planes of walls and ceilings also generates an expansive feeling. Individual lights placed strategically around the room set up overlapping pools of light and shade.

Certain activities call for the additional boost of task-lighting, that is, light directed so it falls on the focus of attention, whether it is a desk, kitchen counter or home workshop. Ceiling mounted spotlights that can be adjusted to target specific areas make good sense where layout is fixed, in kitchens and bathrooms, for example. A related strategy, one that calls for much lower light levels, is to direct a narrow beam of light at whatever you put on display – a collection of ceramics, for example, or a sparkling array of glassware.

Scandinavian Modern Trademarks

Walls and Floors

In the Scandinavian modern interior, walls are conceived as serene backdrops and rarely make a strong decorative statement of their own. In this supporting role, they are often painted white or some other pale, luminous shade, which has the effect of making the most of available light and providing a reticent background against which vivid accent colours sing out. White is not a fail-safe option in the Scandinavian interior, but a positive choice. On a winter's day, it captures every sparkle of light reflected off the dazzling snow. In summer it is cool, crisp and fresh. Its airiness makes rooms seem more spacious than they are and throws the attention onto the sculptural quality of furniture and the interplay of architectural planes.

Where colour is used on walls, it generally takes the form of the natural hues displayed by materials such as wood panelling or stone. Warm, lighter-toned woods such as beech and birch are the Scandinavian preference, while stone is often local granite, honed smooth or in rough-textured blocks. This gentle palette of mid-browns and greys offers textural interest, too, a reminder of the vitality of the natural world.

In keeping with the liveable Scandinavian modern aesthetic, pale is never uninteresting.

Colour does play an important role in the interior, as does pattern. Most often these elements are displayed in rugs, textiles, artwork and decorative objects, which provide visual as well as tangible comfort.

One key colour combination in the Scandinavian interior is blue and white, a favourite pairing that dates back to the eighteenth century and Gustavian style. While blue and white can evoke a homely domesticity, in Scandinavian contexts it is both more elemental and more elegant.

After walls, the floor is the second largest surface area in the interior and as such has a dominant effect on the way we perceive space. What's more, it's a surface with which we constantly interact – how it sounds and how it feels matter just as much as how it looks. At the same time, choice of flooring must deliver basic practicality, particularly in hard-working areas of the home, such as kitchens, bathrooms and hallways.

In the Scandinavian modern interior, flooring provides a clean sweep that enhances the flow of space and serves as a powerful unifier, particularly in open-plan layouts. Where indoors merges with outdoor spaces, the same effect can be achieved if internal flooring and external paving or decking is very similar tonally, even if different materials are used.

Wood, tile and stone are favourite options. Each of these materials offers the potential to set up a subtle rhythm according to format and the pattern of laying. Hardwoods can be laid in strips, wide boards or in intricate geometric parquetry. Laid diagonally, wood flooring makes a room seem more spacious. Tile and stone come in a range of sizes and can be installed in regular grids, staggered rows or in a more random arrangement. In Jacobsen's own house, he tiled the entire ground floor in ceramic tile laid in a bold graphic grid.

Rarely are rooms carpeted wall-to-wall. Instead vivid rugs deliver comfort underfoot or provide a visual anchor for furniture arrangement.

LEFT A sympathetic palette of materials: warm wood-clad ceiling and pale boards contrast with plain plastered walls, while wallpaper makes a decorative statement.

ABOVE Wood is a defining element of the Scandinavian interior. Here it has been used to clad the walls in snug flush panels.

Furniture

The very essence of Scandinavian modern is the unique family of furniture designs that emerged during the heyday of the style, an impressive number of which are still in production. While modernist classics such as Le Corbusier's chaise longue or 'Grand Confort' armchair (co-designed with Charlotte Perriand), Mies van der Rohe's iconic 'Barcelona' chair or Marcel Breuer's 'Cesca' chair make their bold machine-age proclamations in tubular steel and leather, Scandinavian furniture was largely produced in wood with textile upholstery, which immediately gave it a greater degree of warmth and liveability. In addition to native species such as birch, beech and pine, imported tropical hardwoods were also employed. Teak, in particular, became a visual signature for the style.

Wood was a natural choice for Scandinavian designers in more ways than one. First it was readily accessible; second, there was a long and distinguished craft tradition of working in wood to draw upon. Designers working in the Scandinavian modern idiom, notably the Danes, were able to devise ingenious jointing techniques that allowed separate members such as backs, arms and legs to read as a single, fluid whole. This allowed the supporting frameworks to be revealed in all their elegant simplicity, an honesty fully consonant with modernism.

LEFT Jacobsen's 'Series 7' chairs are one of the most successful designs of all time. Here they make a companionable grouping round a dining table.

BELOW Another iconic Jacobsen design is the 'Grand Prix' chair, with its striking cross-shaped back.

While Scandinavian furniture designers adhered to the same 'form follows function' credo of other early modernists, they instinctively extended the meaning of function to include certain intangible human qualities that broadened the appeal of their pieces and eventually ensured the worldwide success of the style. Practicality and fitness for purpose have always been highly valued in Nordic craft and design, and Scandinavian modern takes fitness for purpose as a given. What makes the designs so approachable, however, is that they deliver practicality without ever losing sight of the fact that furniture is used by human beings. Many modernist chairs are sculptural essays; some are remarkably uncomfortable, or comfortable only in one position. Scandinavian furniture accepts and accommodates the human body in different postures: it's never dictatorial. That is not to say that Scandinavian modern

furniture represents a watering down of modernist ideals. Rather, it combines a modernist clarity of thought with a natural sensibility expressed in curves and flowing forms.

Another key trend that was widely taken up in Scandinavia mid-century was modular furniture. The concept of modular furniture was pioneered earlier in the century by the Bauhaus, where standardised designs were seen to be the solution to producing affordable, functional furniture for everyone. Later, in the 1920s the notion of standardisation was further developed by Le Corbusier and Charlotte Perriand. Corbusier's vision of the modernist interior focused on built-in fittings, modular cabinets and what he called 'type-furniture', that is pieces such as tables and chairs distilled down to their essence. His simple, lightweight metal-framed tables, for example, could be put together in combination according to need and did away with the traditional stylistic conventions that specified different forms for different uses. Equally innovative were his modular storage cabinets or casiers, influenced both by contemporary office furniture and by the 'Innovation' trunk; these also could be put together in different combinations, or used as spatial dividers.

In Scandinavia, modular furniture and modular storage systems became a popular way of addressing the need for space saving and flexibility of use in the interior. Open shelving systems, which can be adjusted to accommodate desks and closed cabinets, have long been part of the Scandinavian modern approach to storage. A key example is the 'String' shelving system designed by Nisse Strinning in 1949, a multi-purpose wall-mounted solution for organising everyday clutter. Similar are other flexible designs, such as tables that can be extended to allow for more place settings when entertaining, or modular seating that permits different configurations. Alvar Aalto's stool, designed in 1932, is the epitome of what Corbusier would have called 'type-furniture'. Serving as a seat, an occasional or bedside table, stackable and mass-produced, this simple

ABOVE Finnish designer Thomas Sandell's 'Snow' cabinet storage system was designed in 1993. Sandell is one of the designers who has worked with IKEA on their 'PS' range. The blanket on the bed is the 'Cross' blanket designed by Swedish designer Pia Wallén. Both are new classics of Scandinavian modern.

stool is all-purpose design at its best, and still contemporary looking over three-quarters of a century after it was first conceived.

Another Scandinavian designer particularly noted for modular design was the Danish architect Jørn Utzon. Best-known for the iconic Sydney Opera House, in the mid-1960s Utzon designed a range of modular furniture for the manufacturer Fritz Hansen. The 'Floating Dock' collection of tables and chairs was based on an interlocking system of triangular-section aluminium components.

Built-in storage has also been a feature of Scandinavian homes for many years. Funkis designers, streamlining the interior into a

functional, multi-purpose space, drew on vernacular antecedents, whereby houses were fitted out as efficiently as possible to make the most of available resources and space. Over the years, this has evolved into a seamless integration of cupboards and storage areas within the architectural framework, so that everyday objects and basic household equipment can be kept out of view.

The Scandinavian modern interior has a strong horizontal emphasis. Furniture is lower, lighter and more compact than traditional designs, a practical bonus that appealed to post-war consumers who generally had less space at

LEFT Neat integrated storage has long been a feature of the Scandinavian interior. The space under the sloping plane of the roof has been fitted with stepped cupboards.

BELOW A similar approach sees larder cupboards slotted alongside a stainless steel fridge in a compact kitchen arrangement.

their disposal than their parents' generation. Many pieces were designed to be part-assembled on site, a trend taken to its furthest extreme today by the flat-pack giant IKEA.

With split-level or open plan layouts, and built-in storage housing clutter, furniture placement often becomes the most important means of signifying distinct areas of activity – a dining area defined by a table and dining chairs, for example, or a living area spelled out in an arrangement of seat furniture and low tables. Scandinavian modern furniture looks supremely natural in such groups – the pieces seem to relate to one another in a comfortable rather than a forced way, chiefly because they are not overwhelmingly rectilinear. And because many of the designs, most notably chairs, have such engaging 'personalities', rooms retain a certain animated quality even when unoccupied.

Textiles

Textiles of all descriptions – hangings, rugs, blankets and upholstery – are vehicles for expressing colour, pattern and warmth in the Scandinavian modern interior. As ever, designs display a blend of modernist abstraction and natural inspiration, a fertile meeting ground between traditional and contemporary. Scandinavia has a long and rich tradition of textile-making, much of it based in the home, with weaving and rug-making skills handed down the generations. Fine yarns were often in short supply, and homespun linen or woollen fabrics were more typical than those made of silk.

One classic Scandinavian textile, which became much associated with Scandinavian modern in its early days, is the Finnish rya (ryiiy) rug. Rya literally means 'shaggy'; these rugs are traditionally knotted onto a backing, leaving a length of yarn to make the nap. Keeping out the cold is a key concern in Nordic regions and ryas were originally used as sleigh rugs or bedding, with the nap side next to the skin. Later they were often given as wedding gifts and hung on the wall.

Other simple handmade rugs, such as runners made from rags or other flatweave carpets, have also been a feature of the Scandinavian interior for a long time. These were often laid to make pathways on bare floorboards, their exuberant stripy patterns adding a touch of homely cheer. Similar flatweave or rag rug designs are widely available today and make a fitting accompaniment to the style, as well as a highly economical one.

In the Scandinavian modern interior, rugs serve as focal points, delivering extra comfort where it is needed, as well as a visual anchor for furniture arrangement. Texture adds an important dimension.

Many Scandinavian modern furniture designs are upholstered, typically in plain coloured wool. In Arne Jacobsen's seat furniture, the close-fitting fine wool upholstery accentuates the organic curves of the designs – making the fabric fit snugly was a particular production challenge. In upholstered furniture by other designers, the wool weave is coarser, more overtly textured and, in practical terms, exceptionally durable.

When Scandinavian modern designs were first exhibited around the world in the 1950s, the work of Danish textile designer and artist Lis Ahlmann attracted much attention. Her simple geometric designs and abstracted organic motifs were executed in a palette of subtle natural shades and became highly influential.

Another international success story was the Finnish textile company Marimekko. Founded in 1951 in Helsinki to address the postwar fabric and clothing shortage in Finland, the company struggled in its early years, but was set on a sound footing after its designs won great acclaim at the 1958 World's Fair in Brussels. Notable Marimekko designers at this time were Maija Isola, Vuokko Eskolin-Nurmesniemi and Annika Rimala. Prints were bold, brightly coloured and youthful, and clothing ranges, produced in 100% cotton, displayed strong, simple shapes. The profile of the company received a significant boost when Jackie Kennedy bought Marimekko dresses during her husband's presidential campaign. Today, Marimekko textiles are more often used as soft furnishings or displayed prominently on the wall as hangings.

ABOVE Marimekko's hugely successful 'Unikko' (Poppy) print brings a splash of vivid colour to a bedroom.

Details

Scandinavian modern never neglects the detail in favour of the big picture. A particular feature of the style is the attention paid to what one might call the accessories of living – glassware, tableware, cutlery, cooking vessels, ice buckets – items that are handled and used every day. Aficionados of Scandinavian modern gain satisfaction from the fact that they can furnish their homes down to the last detail with sympathetic pieces conceived in the same sensibility.

Both decorative and more everyday objects produced in the Scandinavian modern idiom exhibit a delicate poise between sculptural form and basic practicality. This is not surprising. While the Funkis style directed attention at utility and economy, and produced new streamlined shapes, many of the designers and craftspeople working in glass, ceramics and metalware drew on a more expressive tradition that elevated such media to the status of art. Scandinavian modern in many ways represents a reconciliation of the two approaches.

Another hallmark of the style is an instinctive appreciation of different materials, how they are worked and the unique possibilities they provide for form. The designs seem to bring out what each material has to say and capture its essence – glass is never more delicate, ceramics are never more sensuous – an expressiveness that is an obvious outcome of the long craft traditions that exist in these countries. At the same time the unity of the style reflects a certain creative cross-fertilisation. Many Scandinavian modern designers produced work in many different materials – a designer noted for ceramics, for example, might also produce glassware, or a designer noted for work in metal, might also design ceramics.

Glassware is one area in which Scandinavian designers and artists have

excelled. The work of Sven Palmqvist for the Swedish company Orrefors, or Per Lütken's classically simple designs for the Danish glassworks Holmegaard are cases in point. However, by the 1950s Finnish glass was even more acclaimed internationally, particularly designs by Tapio Wirkkala and Timo Sarpaneva.

Many examples of Finnish glass, such as Aino Aalto's rippled tumblers and glassware, first designed in 1932, and still made by Iittala, have since become classics of contemporary design. The 'Wave View' (Bolgeblick) series, later renamed 'Aalto', is made of pressed glass. The ribbed or rippled surface was intended to disguise imperfections arising out of its means of manufacture. While 'Bolgeblick' was conceived as utility glassware, the tactility and solidity of the individual pieces spells out a message of quality and pleasure in use. Equally evocative is the iconic 'Savoy' vase designed by Aino's husband Alvar four years later, with its sinuous organic curves recalling wave-like forms.

Scandinavian ceramics show a similar blend of practicality and artistic sensibility. A successor to Wilhelm Kåge at the Swedish ceramic company Gustavsberg, Stig Lindberg produced asymmetric organic forms that epitomised the direction that Scandinavian modern took in the postwar period. Many of his designs for homewares, such as teapots and vases, were decorated with stylised patterns drawn from nature or folk art.

In the field of metalware, the Danish company founded by Georg Jensen has world renown. Much of the company's output was and remains fine silver jewellery but other products included flatware and table accessories such as jugs and serving dishes, some of which are in stainless steel. Henning Koppel, a designer who had a long association with Georg Jensen, perfected a sculptural, organic visual language both in his designs for jewellery and for bowls, cutlery and dishes.

After the war, the seminal company, Dansk Designs, produced and marketed many

OPPOSITE In the Scandinavian modern aesthetic, everyday objects are both functional and sculptural – worthy of display.

BELOW The focal point in many Scandinavian homes is the hearth, typically a wood-burning stove or open fireplace.

ABOVE Many Scandinavian designers have created objects for mass production as well as one-off art pieces; the two disciplines inform each other.

homewares in the Scandinavian modern style. Dansk was founded in 1954 by Jens Quistgaard, a former student of Georg Jensen, and American entrepreneur, Ted Nierenberg. During their thirty-year partnership, Quistgaard was responsible for designing most of the company's output.

As a designer of everyday products, Quistgaard is notable for his instinctive appreciation of the inherent qualities of different materials and his expressive, organic forms. Many of his best-known and most sought-after designs, including ice buckets, salad bowls and peppermills are made of wood, particularly teak, but he has also

designed cookware, candle holders and cutlery in a range of other materials, including enamelled steel and cast-iron. Blending traditional craftsmanship and forms with a fluid, sculptural approach, Quistgaard's mass-produced domestic products retain an enduring human quality.

The sheer range of designs produced by Scandinavian modern designers spells out an integrated approach to living. This is never more evident than in the work of Arne Jacobsen, whose prolific output included not only buildings and furniture, but light fittings, cutlery, taps and bathroom fittings. His 'AJ' door handle, designed in 1956, and available in matt polished brass or brushed steel, is a furled lever whose form recalls an aeroplane propeller – it seems to invite the hand to engage with it.

It is in the realm of these details that Scandinavian modern truly shows it human side. While the vogue for minimalism, which swept chic interiors bare in the 1990s, represents the furthest extreme of the modernist credo 'less is more' Scandinavian modern has never been severe or self-denying. In a minimalist interior, reduced to the barest of essentials, the humblest object screams for attention, simply because there is little else to look at. Scandinavian modern is far from a cluttered look, but amongst the restraint there is also delight for the eye to rest upon – the pure transparency of glassware, glowing with colour, sinuous organic forms in metal or ceramic, and subtle patterns infused with wit and charm.

RIGHT Vivid glass beakers by the celebrated Finnish designer Kaj Franck are an example of how the Scandinavian aesthetic is able to imbue everyday objects with timeless beauty.

SCANDINAVIAN
MODERN TODAY

BELOW The rectilinear extension is clad in Cor-Ten steel, which will weather to match the cedar siding of the cottage.

New York Cottage Addition

HOME OF BRIAN MESSANA AND TOBY O'RORKE,
COLUMBIA COUNTY, NEW YORK

Dating back to the 1730s, this Dutch settler's house in upstate New York had been much neglected over the years. When the owners bought the property they set about stripping back various partitions and additions to reveal the underlying form of the house, which had all the naïve simplicity of a child's drawing. The bent-frame structure, made out of huge hand-hewn timbers, along with some wide board flooring, and a wattle and daub wall in the fieldstone basement were all that remained of the original building.

OLD AND NEW

The design brief was to renovate the cottage and extend its accommodation in a way that respected the original form while providing contemporary living space. The simple clean lines of the design were inspired by the fortitude of the early settlers, who endured Spartan living conditions as they established their homesteads. The plain rectilinear form of the addition, reminiscent of the trailer homes that are common in the area, provides a strong but complementary foil to the main house. The finish of its external walls, clad in Cor-Ten steel, will eventually weather to the same tone as the wide board cedar siding on the cottage.

The house is where the main living areas are: two bedrooms and a bathroom upstairs and a living room and dining room downstairs separated by a through-wall fireplace. The addition contains the kitchen, a guest bedroom and shower on the ground floor.

MATERIAL QUALITY

A shared palette of interior finishes helps to integrate the cottage with its addition. Only about a third of the original flooring was left and extensive searching turned up nothing compatible. Then out of the blue 1,400 square feet of eighteenth-century wide board flooring turned up at a local antique shop, having been

BELOW Hans Wegner 'Wishbone' chairs surround a dining table made of planks of brut maple mounted on trestles.

LEFT The kitchen, located in the extension, features stainless steel units encased in American walnut. The flooring is limestone.

BELOW A through-wall fireplace separates the living and dining rooms. Furniture is comfortable modular sofas.
OPPOSITE A Wegner 'CH25' armchair in the main bedroom – clean modern lines, superb craftsmanship and the beauty of wood.
OVERLEAF The main bedroom has limestone flooring.

salvaged from a demolished house. This was installed in the cottage, while the flooring in the addition is limestone, also used for the hearth of the central fireplace. Other materials are plaster, exposed oiled wood and stainless steel.

NATURAL SETTING

While the cottage windows are traditional sashes, the addition is extensively glazed in double-insulated glass, blending interior with exterior and providing views of the surrounding apple orchard. Furnishings are a blend of classic contemporary pieces with one-off locally crafted designs, a successful juxtaposition of nature, tradition and modernity that characterises the house as a whole.

BELOW Enormous picture windows were installed during the renovation of the summerhouse.

Danish Summer House

HOME OF KASPER FELDT, COPENHAGEN

An old summerhouse, situated on the coast north of Copenhagen, has been completely renovated by Kasper Feldt, a set designer, to provide a light and airy retreat in tune with its natural setting. Acting as his own architect, Feldt took six months to transform the house into a stunning light-filled pavilion that serves as a showcase for an evolving collection of contemporary furniture and furnishings.

OPENING UP

A key consideration was to open up the house as much as possible in order to connect with the surrounding countryside – the summerhouse is only a short distance from the sea. To this end, Feldt knocked down internal walls that previously divided the space unnecessarily and installed enormous picture windows along two walls.

These windows, which run floor-to-ceiling, pivot 180 degrees to allow a seamless connection with outdoor areas as well as fresh and breezy natural ventilation. The open-plan living/dining area, which includes a compact galley kitchen minimally partitioned from the main space, is the focus of the spatial layout. Feldt redesigned the fireplace, which is inset into a wall. A large decked terrace extends the living area into the garden.

NATURAL PALETTE

From every part of the interior, the surrounding countryside, with its lush vibrant greens, is on show. So as not to detract from the views, the decorative palette is deliberately restrained. The interior has been completely whitewashed to make the most of natural light. Black and brown provide graphic contrast, while turquoise makes

BELOW Extensive decking and a generous table maximise the opportunities for outdoor living and eating.

ABOVE Each section of floor-to-ceiling window pivots 180 degrees to connect house and garden seamlessly and provide a flow of natural ventilation. Feldt bought the bedcover and cushions in India. The reindeer-skin rug came from Iceland.

BELOW A view of the main living area, showing the inset fireplace redesigned by Feldt. The kitchen is minimally separated from the living/dining area and consists of two banks of base units. The kitchen floor is polished black concrete.

a soothing complement to the natural colours of the vegetation and introduces a note of contemporary chic.

MODERN COLLECTION

The pared-down interior, with its sweeping natural views, makes the perfect foil for an eclectic collection of mid-twentieth century furniture, most of which Feldt has picked up for a song in flea markets and other vintage outlets. Pride of place goes to Arne Jacobsen's 'Grand Prix' chairs, designed for Fritz Hansen and now discontinued, which surround the dining table that Feldt himself designed. Other notable pieces include Peter Hvidt's 'AX' chairs, also manufactured by Fritz Hansen and now discontinued. These are grouped around a secondhand coffee table with a white laminate top.

OPPOSITE The dining table was designed by Feldt. Surrounding it are vintage Jacobsen chairs, now discontinued. The oversized pendant light, 'Round Boon', is a contemporary design by Piet Boon for Moooi.

RIGHT The bedroom has a graphic black and white colour scheme. Throughout the house, vintage pieces sit alongside modern finds.

BELOW A daybed by Børge Mogensen sits underneath a 1950s linen hanging by Viola Grasten, a contemporary of Astrid Sampe. The cabinet to the left is a very rare Swedish design.

Swedish Apartment

HOME OF MAGNUS STENSTRÖM, KARLSKRONA, SWEDEN

What began as a hobby back in the mid 1970s has now turned into a livelihood for Magnus Stenström, who opened his shop, Movement Retro Design in Karlskrona nearly ten years ago. Magnus' passion for mid-century design began while he was working in Stockholm. Many of the upmarket restaurants where he was employed were furnished with classic designs by well-known names such as Charles and Ray Eames and Finnish-American architect Eero Saarinen and he became fascinated by the period. Over the years, Magnus' interest has focused more specifically on the work of Danish furniture designers of the 1950s, notably Hans Wegner, Finn Juhl and Børge Mogensen, work he values for the high quality of its craftsmanship, sculptural form and clean modern lines. His apartment in Karlskrona is furnished with the fruits of his collecting, chiefly pieces by Mogensen and almost all of these in oak.

RESTORATION

Magnus sources most of his furniture, both for the shop and his apartment, from Denmark. Although Danish modern furniture is well-known for the quality of its craftsmanship, not all of the designs he has found were in a good state of repair. Sometimes he has been able to restore pieces himself, repairing the oak finish with antique wax. Others have been carefully renovated by a specialist carpenter. However, Magnus is always careful not to overdo the restoration work, believing that you have to see that the pieces are old and carry their own history and originality.

In the living room, a daybed by Mogensen sits beneath a linen hanging by noted Swedish textile designer Viola Grasten. Grasten, a

BELOW A teak bowl by Jens Quistgaard sits on top of the oak cabinet.

LEFT The chest is a very early piece by Mogensen and dates from the 1940s.

ABOVE The cabinet and writing desk are also by Mogensen. The 1940s clock is Danish, as are the ceramics.

OPPOSITE Furniture in Magnus' shop includes 'Series 7' chairs by Jacobsen and a mirror by Luxus, a famous Swedish company founded in the 1950s.

contemporary of Astrid Sampe, was one of those who contributed to the range of 'signed textiles' that Sampe initiated at the Stockholm department store NK during the mid 1950s. The oak cabinet is a very rare Swedish piece. On top is a teak bowl by Jens Quistgaard. On the other side of the living room is a low chest, an old piece by Mogensen that dates from the 1940s and that once belonged to a famous Danish actor. On the wall above is a folding chair.

IN HARMONY

With so many of the pieces of furniture in the apartment being the work of the same designer, from the same period and in the same material,

a natural harmony is built into the picture. The plain white walls and oak parquet floor keep the emphasis on the simple clean lines of the designs. Most of the decorative objects, including ceramics and the 1940s clock on top of the Mogensen cabinet in the study, are Danish.

By the late 1990s Magnus decided it was time to turn his passion into a means of making a living and that was when he opened his Karlskrona shop. Items currently for sale include a brown leather Danish sofa, four Jacobsen 'Series 7' chairs dating from the 1970s and a circular mirror manufactured by the Swedish company Luxus, founded in 1950 and famous for its beautiful lighting and furniture designs.

BELOW LEFT The exterior of the house.
BELOW RIGHT A pendant by Bonnerup, a flea-market find, hangs in the living room, which is simply furnished by pieces from IKEA's PS range. The floor is oak parquet.

London Townhouse

HOME OF LOUISE MUNCH AND GILES MARTIN, LONDON

The owners of this North London late Victorian house are both architects who met when they were working in Berlin. He is English and she is Danish. When they bought the house it was in relatively poor condition and needed quite a lot of work doing to it. At the same time, their budget was limited and careful consideration had to go into making the most of available resources.

SPACE AND LIGHT

A number of alterations were carried out to provide the sense of space that the owners wanted. The dividing wall between the two reception rooms was removed to create an informal family living area. The kitchen, which was tiny, and so low Giles could not stand up in it, was completely rebuilt and extended. To get the necessary head height, they dug down. Three sets of glazed doors were put in, allowing the interior to merge with the exterior. Upstairs, by contrast, the bathroom was very large and included the boiler and an airing cupboard. This was divided into a small separate w.c., where the boiler was repositioned, and a main bathroom. Doors lead out onto a balcony – the house is not overlooked at the rear.

Another key strategy was to repeat materials and finishes throughout. The oak parquet floor in the living room is echoed by the oak veneered kitchen table and solid oak counter, while the slate tiles in the kitchen also crop up in the bathroom shelving. The original timber floors upstairs were sanded and then finished in a traditional Danish fashion – first wood lye was applied to bleach them and then they were washed with a mixture of soap flakes and clay, which both seals the wood and gives it a soft, silky finish.

LEFT The main bathroom is tiled in white and leads onto a balcony. The black Jacobsen 'Ant' chair is one of a number of originals that came from Louise's family home.

ABOVE The extended kitchen includes an eating area. A Henningsen pendant hangs over the simple oak-veneered table. The white chair in the foreground is 'Seagull' by Jacobsen, a design that is no longer in production. The other chairs are white 'Ant' chairs

BELOW The kitchen units are by IKEA; the counter is solid oak. Black slate is used for the kitchen flooring.

FLEA-MARKET TREASURES AND FAMILY HEIRLOOMS

With most of the budget going on building work and a family of young children, spending money on furniture was not a priority. Yet the owners have created a classic contemporary look by combining family antiques with Scandinavian modern classics, some of which came from Louise's parents. Louise's mother has always been a devotee of flea markets. The pendant shade in the living room by Danish architect Claus Bonnerup was found by her. It was subsequently sprayed red with car lacquer. The black 'Ant' chairs by Arne Jacobsen are originals and also come from Louise's family home, as does the kitchen table, part of a Danish range of simple functional furniture dating from the 1950s.

Pride of place goes to the 'Contrast' lamp by Poul Henningsen which hangs over the table and which was once owned by Louise's aunt. Designed in 1958, this light is no longer in production. Neither are the 'Seagull' chairs by Jacobsen, also from Louise's mother – the refinement of the design proved too much for the tensile strength of moulded plywood and because the chairs kept breaking, production was stopped. Two of these are used as dining chairs, along with white 'Ant' chairs.

OPPOSITE A graphic contrast of black and white in the main bedroom. The floorboards were sanded, bleached and then washed with soap and clay, a traditional Danish finish.

BELOW View of the house from the garden. Easy connections with outdoor areas are a feature of Span houses.

Span House

HOME OF CHARLIE MCKEITH AND MADELEINE ADAMS, BLACKHEATH, LONDON

An open secret amongst architects and enthusiasts of modern design, Span developments, largely built in the 1950s and 1960s, remain the perfect model of how to create successful communities and meet housing needs. Designed by one of Britain's most respected architects, Eric Lyons, often in conjunction with landscape architect Ivor Cunningham, the estates were planned around a shared landscape, with the aim of creating communities that interacted naturally: the placing of the buildings with respect to each other and the management of the estates were crucial in achieving that goal. Lyons, influenced by Walter Gropius, was a modernist and the clean contemporary style of Span houses was radical in its day. Between 1948 and 1969 Span built over 2,100 homes, largely in and around London and the southeast.

CLARITY AND BRIGHTNESS

Architects Charlie McKeith and Madeleine Adams have lived in Span houses for 12 years. When they rented their first Span house, they

were not especially aware of the reputation these developments have in design circles. Instead, they were instantly impressed by the simplicity, brightness and provision of space, which although no greater than the average terrace, felt much bigger. They were influenced, too, by the reaction of their year-old daughter, who ran around laughing with delight. A couple of years later they were able to buy their own Span house, which rarely come on the market. Aside from redoing the kitchen and removing a wall that had replaced what had originally been open cabinets, they have had to do very little to it. Over the years, they have increasingly appreciated the special quality of these estates: the fact that they foster contact with neighbours through the shared landscape.

Lyons was an innovator and especially keen on new technologies and materials, which he put into his houses. One feature of many Span houses of this period (early 1960s) is electric underfloor heating. This proved not so successful as the estates themselves and most owners have now disconnected it.

CONTEMPORARY LIVING

Span houses do not impose a particular aesthetic on those who live in them. However, when the owners moved in they already had an eclectic collection of modernist pieces, some inherited and others acquired from a variety of sources. Designs by Arne Jacobsen, Hans Wegner, Charles and Ray Eames and Le Corbusier sit happily together in a comfortable expression of mid-century modern.

PREVIOUS PAGE The house is furnished with a mixture of modern classics, including Jacobsen's 'Egg' chair and Corbusier's 'Grand Confort' sofa. The sideboard was inherited from Madeleine's grandfather.

ABOVE The dentist's chair was found in a junkshop in Blackpool. The flooring is the original parquet.

OPPOSITE The Wegner dining table and three-legged chairs that accompany it were advertised in a local newsagents' window by a family who also lived in a Span house and had bought them new in the 1960s. Other chairs include a cream Eames original, a new Eames chair with 'Eiffel' base and a Panton chair.

BELOW The award-winning house has extensive gardens and a swimming pool.

Retro Home

HOME OF HELEN AND
RICHARD SOMOGYVARI,
JOHANNESBURG,
SOUTH AFRICA

After many visits to the country, Swedish couple Helen and Richard Somogyvari decided to move to South Africa permanently in the late 1990s. While Helen, a designer, was packing up their apartment in Malmö, Richard, who has an online travel business, went househunting in Johannesburg. This 1970s house, in the northern suburb of Randburg, was the first he saw and they both fell in love with its style and expansive rooms. Although they felt obliged to keep looking for a while, it was this house that they eventually bought.

CONTEMPORARY STYLE

The winner of an architectural award, the house is arranged so that every room embraces the garden, reinforcing an easy-going indoors/outdoors lifestyle. It needed relatively little renovation. Fortunately all the internal wooden

detailing – panelled walls, ceilings, shelves and shutters – was in the original unpainted condition, making a perfect retro backdrop for the couple's Swedish modern furnishings.

The only building work required was to knock through into the kitchen to create an inclusive open-plan space. Tiles were also taken up from the floor and a concrete screed added, which was subsequently painted grey. Helen was able to source the same red tiles in the bathroom, an original feature, to use on the patio.

MIX AND MATCH

The house is furnished with a variety of contemporary pieces that the couple brought from Sweden. Amongst basics from IKEA, such as the living room sofas, and junk-shop finds are designer pieces that Helen chiefly acquired from Davies in Sweden, where she once worked.

LEFT The dining chairs are Jacobsen 'Series 7' chairs; the table is made of South African wood and the pendant is a Le Klint shade. The wooden ceilings and panelling are in their original unpainted finish.

BELOW 'Unikko' fabric, designed by Maija Isola for Marimekko, is one of the vivid colour accents in the house.

Arne Jacobsen's 'Series 7' chairs in white surround a dining table made out of South African wood. The Le Klint folded paper lampshade, first produced in the 1940s, is a Scandinavian modern classic.

COLOUR

A particular feature of the interior is the use of strong colour. Helen, who designs handbags and soft furnishings from her home-based studio, is an avid collector of textiles, amongst other things. Throughout the house brilliant injections of bold colour sing out against the wood-lined walls. In the kitchen, an array of intensely coloured glassware is backlit by a window in opaque glass, while Marimekko's 'Unikko' (Poppy) print is used as a vivid bedcover.

ABOVE The living area is bathed in
natural light that spills in through large
picture windows. The chairs were junk
shop finds, reupholstered by Helen.

OPPOSITE In the living room is a pair
of IKEA sofas accessorised with cushions
made up in a retro fabric found in
Sweden. The flokati rug was bought in
South Africa, while the sideboard is a
1970s Swedish design.

BELOW The house is beautifully integrated into its sloping site, raised on a plinth with exterior terraces.

BELOW The house is beautifully integrated into its sloping site, raised on a plinth with exterior terraces.

Modern masterpiece

FORMERLY THE HOME OF
POVL AND BIRGIT AHM,
HARPENDEN, HERTFORDSHIRE

Grade II-listed and described by English Heritage as 'distinguished and beautifully detailed', this superb modern house is the product of a collaboration between Jørn Utzon and Povl Ahm, a hugely talented Danish engineer who assisted Utzon in the development of Sydney Opera House, as he had previously assisted Basil Spence at Coventry Cathedral and Arne Jacobsen at St Catherine's College, Oxford. Ahm was working in London for Ove Arup when he acquired the sloping site for the house. He sent plans and photographs to Utzon in Denmark, who came up with the scheme. Then Ahm, who in later years would become chairman of Arup, spent two years realising the project, cutting no corners in its construction and paying loving attention to every detail.

SPATIAL PROGRESSION

One of the key features of the design is the sense of spatial progression. A long low porch lets into an entrance hall. Wide steps lead up to the main living area with its two flanking walls glazed floor to ceiling and then up again to the dining area and kitchen. Swedish Hoganas tiles, similar to those used in the Sydney Opera House, are used for flooring throughout, extending out onto the terraces and reinforcing the blurring of boundaries between indoors and out. One of the features of the house, radical in its day, is the hot-water underfloor heating, which means the free-flowing spaces are not interrupted by radiators.

TIMELESS DESIGN

An aspect of the house that has given it an enduring modernity is the palette of materials. In addition to the tiling and the extensive use of glazing, there are great exposed polished precast concrete beams, walls and a fireplace of

ABOVE A view from the living area up wide shallow steps to the dining area. The rectangular hatch connects to the kitchen at the heart of the house.

LEFT The sloping roof of the building is faced in copper. Extensive glazing brings warm south light into the living areas.

pale yellow London brick, doors and ceilings made of Oregon pine. The window mullions are teak. All of these are long-lasting, need little or no maintenance and contribute pleasing textural variation, as well as expressing the design and engineering of the structure.

Equally timeless is the collection of furniture acquired by Ahm and his wife Birgit. Pieces by Arne Jacobsen and other Danish contemporaries are arranged throughout the interior. For all the attention to detail and fastidious taste, this is no sterile showcase of modernity; instead it remains a warm, welcoming and light-filled family home.

PREVIOUS PAGES Jacobsen 'Swan' and 'Egg' chairs, upholstered in tan leather, along with other classic Danish modern pieces, furnish the living room.

OPPOSITE View up into the main open-plan living room and dining area.

Resources

IN SCANDINAVIA

ADELTA
Friedrich-Ebert-Str. 96,
D-46535 Dinslaken, Germany
tel +49 2 064 40 797
e adelta@t-online.de
www.adelta.de
Producer of Eero Aarnio designs

ARTEK
Eteläesplanadi 18, 00130
Helsinki, Finland
tel +35 8 961 32 52 77
www.artek.fi
*Established by Aalto to produce
his own furniture*

ASPLUND
Sibyllegatan 31, 11442
Stockholm, Sweden
tel +46 8 662 52 84
www.asplund.org
*Furniture and rugs by designers
including Thomas Sandell and
Pia Wallén*

CARL HANSEN & SØN
Holmevaenget 8, DK-5560
Aarup, Denmark
tel +45 66 12 14 04
e info@carlhansen.dk
www.carlhansen.dk
*Producer of Hans Wegner
designs*

DANSK
PO Box 2006, Bristol,
PA 19007-0806, US
tel +1 800 326 7528
www.dansk.com

DANSK MØBELKUNST
Bredgade 32,
1260 Copenhagen, Denmark
tel +45 33 32 38 37
e info@dmk.dk
www.dmk.dk

ERIK JØRGENSEN
Industrivaenget 1, DK-5700
Svendborg, Denmark
tel +45 62 21 53 00
e info@erik-joergensen.com
www.erik-joergensen.com
*Furniture by designers including
Poul Volther and Hans Wegner*

FREDERICIA
Treldevej 183, DK-7000
Fredericia, Denmark
tel +45 75 92 33 44
e sales@fredericia.com
www.fredericia.com
*Furniture by designers including
Nanna Ditzel*

FRITZ HANSEN
Allerødvej 8, 3450 Allerød,
Denmark
tel +45 48 17 23 00
e @fritzhansen.com
www.fritzhansen.com
*Furniture by designers including
Arne Jacobsen and Poul
Kjærholm*

KNUD HOLSCHER DESIGN
Vermundsgade 40, DK-2100
Copenhagen 40, Denmark
tel +45 39 29 10 01
www.holscherdesign.com
d-line architectural hardware

KVADRAT
Lundbergsvej 10, DK-8400
Ebeltoft, Denmark
tel +45 89 53 18 66

e web@kvadrat.dk
www.kvadrat.dk
Textiles by designers including Arne Jacobsen, Nanna Ditzel and Verner Panton

LE KLINT
Store Kirkestraede 1, DK-1073 København K, Denmark
tel +45 33 11 66 63
e butik@leklint.dk
www.leklint.com
Lighting by designers including Kaare Klint and Hvidt & Mølgaard

LOUIS POULSEN
Gammel Strand 28, DK-1202, Copenhagen, Denmark
tel +45 70 33 14 14
e lpl_international@lpmail.com
www.louispoulsen.com
Lighting by designers including Poul Henningsen, Arne Jacobsen and Verner Panton

MARIMEKKO
www.marimekko.com
Maija Isola's original textiles, plus recent designs. Stores worldwide.

MODERNITY
Sibyllegatan 6,
114 42 Stockholm, Sweden
tel +46 8 20 80 25
e info@modernity.se
www.modernity.se

MOVEMENT RETRO DESIGN
Arklimästaregatan 35,
371 35 Karlskrona, Sweden
tel +45 5 254 43
www.movementdesign.se

NANNA DITZEL
Klareboderne 4, DK-1115 Copenhagen, Denmark
tel +45 33 93 94 80
www.nanna-ditzel-design.dk
Designer of furniture and textiles; available from Fredericia

PP MØBLER
Toftevej 30, DK-3450 Allerød, Denmark
tel +45 48 17 21 06
e info@pp.dk
www.pp.dk
Furniture by designers including Hans Wegner

STELTON AS
PO Box 59, GL. Vartov Vej 1, DK-2900 Hellerup, Denmark
tel +45 3962 3055
e stelton@stelton.dk
www.stelton.com

VOLA
Lunavej 2, DK-8700 Horsens, Denmark
tel +45 70 23 55 00
e sales@vola.dk
en.vola.com
Architectural hardware including taps by Arne Jacobsen

OUTSIDE SCANDINAVIA

HUSET.
www.huset-shop.com

FINNISH DESIGN SHOP
www.finnishdesignshop.com

MID-CENTURY MODERN
www.modernshows.com

THE MODERN WAREHOUSE
www.themodernwarehouse.com

GALERIE DANSK MØBELKUNST
www.dmk.dk

SHANNON
www.shannon-uk.com

SKANDIUM
www.skandium.com

THE LOLLIPOP SHOPPE
www.thelollipopshoppe.com

TWENTYTWENTYONE
www.twentytwentyone.com

Index

Scandinavian Index

Picture Credits

PAGES 2–3 © Tim Crocker www.timcrocker.co.uk; PAGE 5: Ditte Isager www.ditteisager.dk; PAGE 6: Jan Baldwin/Narratives; PAGE 8: www.artek.fi; PAGES 9–13: Åke E:son Lindman; PAGE 14: C.G. Rosenberg, 1930/Artitekturmuseet, Stockholm; PAGE 15: Nyholm, 1939/Artitekturmuseet, Stockholm; PAGES 16–18 Åke E:son Lindman; PAGE 19 TOP: Jørgen Strüwing, BELOW: *Radisson* Radisson SAS Royal Hotel; PAGE 20: Bo Törngren/Artitekturmuseet, Stockholm; PAGE 21: Wilhelm Kåge/Praktika/© The National Museum of Fine Arts; PAGE 22: Eino Mäkinen, Alvar Aalto Museum; PAGE 23: Paul Ryan/Timo Sarpaneva; PAGE 24: Åke E:son Lindman; PAGE 25: Lars Hallen; PAGE 26: Villa Stenersen, Arne Korsmo. Photo: Magnus Aspelin; PAGE 27: Villa Stenersen, Arne Korsmo. Photo: Jiri Havran; PAGE 28: Robert P. Ruschak, Courtesy Western Pennsylvania Conservancy; PAGE 30: Bettman/Corbis; PAGE 31 LEFT: Image courtesy of The Advertising Archives, RIGHT: www.kohlerinteriors.com; PAGE 32: Image courtesy of The Advertising Archives; PAGE 33: Inter IKEA Systems B.V. 2007; PAGE 34: www.artek.fi; PAGE 35: Lars Hallen; PAGES 36–37: Maija Holma, Alvar Aalto Museum; PAGE 38: Lars Hallen; PAGE 40: Maija Holma, Alvar Aalto Museum; PAGE 41: Per Ranung/Linnea Press, Styling: Anna Ranung; PAGE 42: www.artek.fi; PAGE 43 TOP: www.artek.fi, BELOW: Martti Kapanen, Alvar Aalto Museum; PAGE 44 TOP: Martti Kapanen, Alvar Aalto Museum, BELOW: Paul Ryan/Kirsti Paakonen; PAGE 45: www.artek.fi; PAGE 46: Marianna Wahlsten; PAGE 47: Eero Aarnio Archives; PAGES 48–49: www.rosendahl.com; PAGE 50: Lars Hallen; PAGE 51 TOP: Keld Helmer Petersen,1957 www.nanna-ditzel-design.dk; BELOW: www.artek.fi; PAGE 52: www.gense.se; PAGE 53: www.porsgrund.com; PAGES 54–55: www.iittala.com; PAGE 57: Jesper Ray/ House of Pictures; PAGES 58–59: www.louispoulsen.com; PAGE 60: www.dline.com; PAGE 61 © Fritz Hansen/Struwing; PAGE 62: Kennet Havgaard/House of Pictures; PAGES 63–65: © 2008 Marimekko Corporation. All rights reserved; PAGE 66: The Danish National Art Library, The Architectural Drawings Collection; PAGES 67–68: Lars Hallen; PAGE 69: © Fritz Hansen; PAGES 70–71: © Fritz Hansen/Ditte Isager; PAGE 72: Egg Boontje © Fritz Hansen 2006/Egon Gade; PAGE 73: Kim Ahm/House of Pictures; PAGE 74: © Tim Crocker www.timcrocker.co.uk/Design: Julian Cowie Architects; PAGE 75 TOP: © Fritz Hansen 2006/Sven Bruun; BELOW: www.mobach-groothandel.nl; PAGE 76 TOP LEFT & RIGHT: www.louispoulsen.com; BELOW: www.vola.co.uk; PAGE 77 TOP: www.georgjensen.com; BELOW: www.stelton.com; PAGES 78–81: Onecollection A/S www.onecollection.com; PAGE 82: © Fritz Hansen/Egon Gade; PAGE 83: Ditte Isager www.ditteisager.dk; PAGE 84: © Fritz Hansen/Ditte Isager; PAGE 85: © Fritz Hansen/Egon Gade; PAGE 87: www.avarte.fi; PAGE 88: www.ahg.se; PAGE 89: www.designhousestockholm.com; PAGE 90–91: www.holmegaard.com; PAGE 92 TOP: Tim Street-Porter, BELOW & PAGE 93: www.bruno-mathsson-int.se; PAGES 94–95: www.fredericia.com; PAGE 96: Lars Rebers/Design Museum, Finland; PAGE 97: Rauno Traskelin/Design Museum, Finland; PAGE 98: Per Larsson/Orrefors Archive/ www.orrefors.se; PAGE 99: Orrefors Archive/www.orrefors.se; PAGE 100: Jan Baldwin/Narratives; PAGE 101 TOP: Hans Hansen, © Vitra, BELOW: www.louispoulsen.com; PAGE 102 TOP: Jiri Havran/ House of Pictures, BELOW: Hans Hansen, © Vitra; PAGE 103: www.sigurdpersson.se; PAGE 105: Beth Evans; PAGE 106: www.modernshows.com; PAGE 107: Katharine Lazenby; PAGES 109–111: Images courtesy of Knoll Inc. www.knoll.com; PAGE 113: Astrid Sampe, Lazy Lines/© The National Museum of Fine Arts; PAGES 114–115: www.iittala.com; PAGE 116: Jørn Utzon for Lightyears/ www.informfurniture.co.uk; PAGE 117: www.erik-joergensen.com; PAGE 119: Søren Larsen/ www.carlhansen.dk; PAGE 120 LEFT: PP Møbler – pp550, Peacock chair. Credit:

PP Møbler www.pp.dk, RIGHT: PP Møbler – pp19,Teddy Bear chair. Credit: PP Møbler www.pp.dk; PAGE 121 TOP Jan Baldwin/Narratives, BELOW: Søren Larsen/www.carlhansen.dk; PAGE 122 TOP: Paul Ryan, BELOW: PP Møbler – pp501/503, The Chair. Credit: PP Møbler www.pp.dk; PAGE 123 TOP: Kennet Havgaard/House of Pictures, BELOW: PP Møbler – pp589. Bar Bench. Credit: PP Møbler www.pp.dk; PAGE 124: www.iittala.com; PAGE 125: Beth Evans; PAGE 126: Ditte Isager www.ditteisager.dk; PAGE 127: Jan Baldwin/Narratives; PAGE 128–129: Grazia Ike Branco/Interior Designer: Nilla; PAGE 130: Per Ranung/Linnea Press, Styling: Anna Ranung; PAGE 131: Tia Borgsmidt/Linnea Press, Styling: Sidsel Zachariasen; PAGE 132: Lars Hallen; PAGE 133: James Silverman; PAGE 134: Paul Ryan/ Ole Rex Architects; PAGE 135: Paul Ryan; PAGES 136–137: Åke E:son Lindman; PAGE 138: Grazia Ike Branco/Interior Designers: David and Madeleine Carlson; PAGE 139: Paul Ryan/Corinne Calesso; PAGE 140: Birgitte Wolfgang Drejer/House of Pictures; PAGE 141: Kim Ahm/House of Pictures; PAGE 142: Paul Ryan/Michael Asplund; PAGE 143: Paul Ryan/Kastrup & Sjunnesson Architects; PAGE 144: Paul Ryan/Gunnel Sahlin; PAGE 145: Helén Pe/ House of Pictures; PAGE 146: Beth Evans; PAGE 147: Kennet Havgaard/House of Pictures; PAGE 148: Beth Evans; PAGE 149: Jan Baldwin/Narratives; PAGES 150–151: Paul Ryan; PAGES 152–157: Gaelle Le Boulicaut/Messana O'Rorke Architects, New York/Stylist: Jeremy Callaghan; PAGES 158–163: Linnea Press/Lars Ranek; PAGES 164–167: Patric Johansson/House of Pictures; PAGES 168–171: Andreas von Einsiedel; PAGES 172–175: © Tim Crocker www.timcrocker.co.uk; PAGES 176–179: Jan Baldwin/ Narratives; PAGES 180–185: © Tim Crocker www.timcrocker.co.uk; ENDPAPERS: 'Trapez' textile by Arne Jacobsen/Photo: © Casper Sejersen Courtesy of **kvadrat** www.kvadrat.dk

Acknowledgements

As ever, I would like to thank the team at Quadrille for all their hard work and generous support: Anne Furniss for her enthusiasm and belief in the project, Helen Lewis for inspired art direction, Katherine Case for designing the book beautifully and Lisa Pendreigh for her editorial guidance and patient research. My thanks also to Helen Stallion for tracking down the images.